ROMANIA'S COMMUNIST TAKEOVER

THE RĂDESCU GOVERNMENT

ROMANIA'S COMMUNIST TAKEOVER: THE RĂDESCU GOVERNMENT

BY
DINU C. GIURESCU

EAST EUROPEAN MONOGRAPHS, BOULDER
DISTRIBUTED BY COLUMBIA UNIVERSITY PRESS, NEW YORK

1994

EAST EUROPEAN MONOGRAPHS, NO. CCCLXXXVIII

ISBN 0-88033-285-9
Library of Congress Catalog Card Number 94-70331

Printed in the United States of America

ACKNOWLEDGEMENTS

It is a duty and a great pleasure for me to acknowledge my heartfelt thanks to all who in varying ways helped me to complete this work.

My expression of deep gratitude is here reserved for Professor Stephen Fisher-Galaţi who steadily encouraged and helped me to undertake the study and published it in the East European Monographs.

The same gratitude is expressed to my wife Dr. Anca Elena Giurescu who constantly assisted me; and to my daughter Ena Simona Giurescu M.A., who helpfully read the manuscript.

I want to thank the staffs at the National Archives, Washington DC, at the New York Public Library and at the Library of Congress.

I am indebted to Carol Alpert of the New York University, the Library of the School of Law, for all her assistance to my long lasting documentation.

I repeatedly benefited of George Minden's and Ioana Alimăneşteanu's help at the International Book Exchange Fund, Inc. of New York City, N.Y.

Many thanks to my typist Ms. Elise Oiaga.

DINU C. GIURESCU

May 21, 1993

CONTENTS

INTRODUCTION

In October 1943 the Romanian vice-consul in Istanbul approached a British SOE (Special Operation Executive) representative with a plan for a coup d'état in Romania directed in the name of King Mihai and aimed at overthrowing Marshal Antonescu.

Two generals were connected with the plan and they claimed to have officers of all ranks to execute any orders. It was known, however, that some high ranking officers could not be counted upon to join the military uprising.

The movement claimed to have at its disposal some 500,000 men armed with rifles, Bren guns and mortars but deficient in artillery, in tanks and antitank weapons. Iuliu Maniu president of the National Peasant Party and a few other persons were somehow aware of such plans to get Romania out of the war. King Mihai only knew that the movement was organized in his name.

The two leading generals were ready to start the action as soon as the UK government had sent a high-ranking officer with a token force of 1,000 to 2,000 paratroopers on the Eastern front where together with the Soviet command, they would receive the unconditional surrender of the Romanian army.[1]

The spokesman of the group a colonel in command of a regiment in Bucharest, asked for a "high-ranking British Staff Officer" as a liaison officer as well as a wireless set and operator.

The UK reactions to the plan were not encouraging. "The scheme seems at present embryonic and not very hopeful" wrote the British Embassy in Washington DC. The "estimate of 500,000 men seems greatly exaggerated".[2] It was unlikely to find a purely Romanian held sector on the Soviet front where the surrender of the Romanian Army could effectively take place. The plan didn't take into account the proper reactions of the German command and of Marshal Ion Antonescu as well. As for presence of British paratroops, as requested, the move couldn't be done unless the operation is considered "of highest importance" by the Combined Chiefs of Staff.

"In spite of the numerous weaknesses of the scheme, His Majesty Government" wanted to know US Government's views on the subject. The British would not take any initiative beyond "trying to establish wireless contact with the group".[3]

Non committal comments came from the State Department. Almost three months had elapsed since the original proposal was put forward "without bringing any apparent crystallization" of the plan wrote the Memo of the State Department. The absence of any action "tends to throw a doubt on the likelihood of its eventual maturity".[4]

The State Department was wondering why the Romanian military group once it had succeeded to overthrow the Antonescu regime should not send "representatives out of the country to some neutral point... to offer unconditional surrender and to sign the terms therefore before the representatives of the three principal Allies".[5]

The US Joint Chiefs of Staff expressed its opinion similarly: "...the scheme is embryonic and not very hopeful". The lack of apparent crystallization of the plan "seems to make its maturity unlikely".[6]

Admiral William D. Leahy, US Chief of Staff to the Commander in Chief of the Army and Navy, added that "Romania's eventual withdrawal from the war may very possibly follow the basic pattern of the internal uprising as set forth in this proposal".

As a consequence the contact with "dissidents groups" should be maintained as to encourage them "to rise and force the withdrawal of the Romania from the war on the most favourable basis for the Allies".[7] There was not a single word about sending a token military Western force to Romania if the surrender had to be signed on the Eastern Front.

Thus the prospects of the Romanian military coup against the Nazi Reich was considered rather skeptically by the British and US military and diplomatic decision makers. They had experienced the Italian surrender on September 3, 1943, which didn't bring about dramatic changes. The Wehrmacht was able to regain the control of most of the Italian Peninsula and to stabilize the front-line for months to come.

In Romania's case the country was integrated into the main sector of the Eastern battle front and with Wehrmacht units in and around it. Besides the area was vital for the German war effort. From London and Washington DC the chances of a Romanian successful coup seemed therefore very remote, if at all.

The Romanian political and military action started on August 23, 1944, in the afternoon, four days after the Soviet offensive had rapidly developed in Moldavia.

The outcome of the action went far beyond anyone's expectations. Moscow, London and Washington DC were taken totally by surprise.

The B.B.C. was the first to report on the events in the evening. Upon hearing the London radio announcement, Averell Harriman, US Ambassador in Moscow inquired whether "the Soviet Government had any knowledge of this matter further than what had been announced by radio from Bucharest". The Soviet official didn't know anything but promised to transmit the US inquiry "to the higher authorities".[8]

Next day, August 24, in the afternoon, Ambassador A. Harriman called on Vishinsky who stated "that the Soviet authorities had no information whatsoever except what had been heard over the radio and that he had no instructions from his government to make any statement on this matter at the present time".[9]

On August 25, at 3 a.m. Vyaceslaw Molotov told the US and UK ambassadors "that the Soviet Government had waited all day, i.e. August 24, 1944, but so far had received no word from Bucharest except from the public radio broadcast".[10]

In a few days it became obvious that the Romanian Army had succeeded in breaking down all Wehrmacht's resistance within the country. The Soviet army advanced unopposed in full speed whilst the Romanian units kept all the Carpathian passes open and halted all German attempts to establish a new front-line on the mountain's range.

As a consequence of the Romanian events the Wehrmacht's positions in the Balkans disintegrated at a rapid pace from Crete and Greece to Belgrade.

The armistice between Romania and USSR, USA and UK was signed in Moscow on September 12, 1944, some 20 days after the beginning of the Bucharest military action.[11]

In the meanwhile the Soviets had advanced unopposed some 600 miles and had taken over 100,000 Romanian prisoners with the "motivation" that Romania was "juridical" still at war with the USSR.[12]

It is worth remembering the Statement issued by the People's Commissariat of Foreign Affairs, in Moscow, on August 25, 1944: "The Soviet High Command believes if the Romanian armies cease military action against the Red Army and if they join arm in arm with the Red Army carrying in the war of liberation... the Red Army *will not disarm them, will let them keep all their arms and will fully aid them in fulfilling this honorable task*". (my italics, D.C.G.).[13]

The Soviet political authorities were facing a new situation with regard to Romania in August 1944. They had expected to gradually conquer the country and to set in a provisional administration or to sign an armistice with Marshal Antonescu and to proceed from this point.

The Romanian government had not emerged under the Soviet occupation, but was actually a reaction against Marshal Antonescu's leadership. Hastily organized on the evening of August 23rd, 1944, and headed by General Constantin Sănătescu, the new government had the political backing of the National Democratic Bloc which included the

National Peasants, the National Liberals, the Social Democrats, and the Communist Party of Romania, i.e. all political forces opposed to the German alliance.

Moreover the Sănătescu cabinet moved rapidly toward a constitutional parliamentary regime.

By royal decree the citizens' rights and the state powers were reinstated according to the provisions of the 1866 and 1923 Constitutions.[14] The aim was to get Romania back to a constitutional monarchical regime as before 1938 with elections to be organized at the first opportunity.[15]

The Soviets had opposite views, namely to eventually impose a communist regime in Romania as elsewhere in other East European "liberated" countries.

Moscow had one powerful essential tool at disposal. The Red Army had occupied the country to an extent never imagined during the German predominance (October 1940 to August 1944). Every major component of the Romanian administration was tightly controlled through the Allied (Soviet) Control Commission instituted by the Armistice Convention.[16] The internal political developments were spearheaded by the Communist Party of Romania which had the full support of the Soviet army and authorities.

In August 1944 the Communist Party of Romania had less than or about 1,000 registered members.[17] Its road to full power started in September 1944 and was completed with the Soviet imposition of the government headed by Dr. Petre Groza on March 6, 1945.

A United Workers' Front was the first move, on September 1, 1944. It was based on an agreement between the communists and social-democrats.[18] Devoid of almost any power base, the communists needed the United Front to control and manipulate the factory workers for the forthcoming staged demonstrations.

The second move was to trigger an artificial political crisis. On September 24, communist leader Gheorghiu Dej asserted that the Sănătescu cabinet had failed to purge the administration of the fascists. Dej requested the formation of a new government representing "the largest urban and rural categories, all democratic forces of the country".[19] The Central Committee of the Communist Party presented the project of a Platform of the National Democratic Front and invited "all democratic forces" to join.[20]

Rallies in the factories and the street demonstration followed in the "support" for the NDF platform. The communist activists of the Unions' Committees "mobilized" the workers. There were many promises and populist slogans for a better life. There was an implicit threat of unemployment if the meetings were not attended.

The procommunist press reported almost daily demonstrations expressing the "people's will" and support for the Platform and a NDF cabinet.[21]

The National Democratic Front included the Communists, the Social Democrats, the Ploughmen Front, the Socialist Peasant Party, the Patriots' Union – a loose group directed by the Communists, the Popular Peasant Party, the United Workers' Front, the National Democratic Front of the Youth, the Union of the Democratic University Students.[22]

Excepting the Social Democrats all the other leftist groups affiliated to the NDF had very limited audience within the potential electorate. In all the NDF had presumably less than 10 per cent support of the popular vote. The Communist street demonstrations and meetings on the public squares or in the stadiums, gathered several thousands participants.[23] They were driven by the populist provisions of the NDF platform and by the activists' technique of mobilization. They hopped for improved living standards. Their "motivation" included their submissive mood to orders, their opportunism, or fear of loosing the job if not joining the manifestation. The pro-communist participants represented five to six percentages of the country's working force,[24] even if the NDF forcefully and vociferously claimed to express the will of the whole people.[25]

The Communist Party wanted a dominant position through the NDF. On October 19, 1944, the press released the NDF proposals for a new cabinet headed by Dr. Petre Groza. Out of eighteen ministers and secretaries of State, eleven (61,1%) were to be NDF, five National Liberals and National Peasants (27,7%), and two (11,2%) neutral. The latter included the Foreign Affairs and the War Department with ministers obviously favourable to the NDF goals.[26]

The proposals offered a token participation to the traditional parties, i.e. National Peasants and Liberals, as a transitional phase to a complete take over. Had it been accepted, the NDF coalition government would have started to nominate the pro-communist people at every level.

The NDF Council addressed the nation in a manifesto which violently blamed and vilified the existing "reactionary" government for all the hardship and misery people were suffering.[27]

In a first phase (October 4–13) the traditional parties stood for the continuation of a coalition cabinet with some main objectives to be agreed on and to be achieved.[28]

In mid October the National Peasant Party expressed its willingness to form a new cabinet either alone or in cooperation with all the parties ready to continue a genuine political coalition.[29] The NPP published its own platform on October 16, 1944, based on the main principles of a pluralist political life, separation of state powers, individual rights and liberties, private property, constitutional monarchy.[30]

A pro-NPP meeting on October 15, was banned by the government at special request of the Allied (Soviet) Control Commission.[31] Throughout the country pro-NPP meetings and rallies took place despite the threats and various intimidation tactics of the communist lead National Democratic Front.[32] On Sunday, October 29, 1944, a meeting took place in the ARO Theater followed by a large street demonstration in Bucharest. The NPP leaders Ion Mihalache and Iuliu Maniu took the floor and explained the party's objectives. The participants approved a motion with specific points centered on the loyal and integral fulfillment of the Armistice Convention.[33]

In a normal political life the communist lead coalition wouldn't have ever succeeded to get a substantial power-sharing. In a country occupied by the Soviets nothing worked however the normal way. The Allied (Soviet) Control Commission (ACC) was a *de facto* super-government which imposed its views at decisive moments.

On November 1, 1944, general Vinogradov, Deputy Chairman of the ACC, presented a written note in the name of the ACC to King Mihai and the Prime Minister demanding the formation of a coalition government headed by General Constantin Sănătescu with Dr. Petre Groza as vice-premier and Lucrețiu Pătrășcanu as Minister of Justice. Iuliu Maniu and C.I.C. Brătianu "were not to be included in the new government".

The UK representative with ACC, Air Vice Marshal Stevenson called on general Vinogradov next day, November 2, 1944, and asked him on his recent interview with the King and the presentation of a note in the name of the ACC *which the British had not seen previously* (my italics D.C.G.). Air Vice Marshal added that if the ACC authority was to be used the British and the US representatives "must be consulted to make such authority valid". General Vinogradov seemed somewhat embarrassed.[34] Understandably the ACC order was maintained.

The same November 1, 1944, Iuliu Maniu sent a message[35] to UK representative in Bucharest, Vice Air Marshal Stevenson. The NPP leader inquired whether the British government intended "to hand over Romania" to the Soviets.[36] As expected, Stevenson's answer was that such a "hand over" intention "was not held by (the) British government".[37] The answer was given by the British representative in Bucharest twenty four days after Churchill and Stalin had agreed on the ninety per cent Soviet dominance in Romania.[38]

The second Sănătescu cabinet was sworn in on November 6, 1944. It lasted 27 days. The ratio of forces was eight ministers of the National Peasant and Liberal parties to seven NDF, communists or affiliated. The Prime minister was General Constantin Sănătescu whilst the Vice-premier was the pro-communist Dr. Petre Groza.[39] The Communist Party couldn't control the ministries of the Interior and of the War. Due to the direct Soviet intervention the Communist Party had however made a very important step on the road to a complete take over.

After mid November, the NDF launched a new campaign of public disobedience, of demonstrations aimed at unsettling and eventually dislodge the government. Any pretext was good. The legal local administration started to be dismissed by communist lead mobs. The "motivation" was the "purge of the fascists" and the "democratization" of the state institutions. Prefects and/or mayors replaced through "popular will" in Constanţa, Brăila, Arad, Griviţa (a suburb of Bucharest), Ploieşti, Tîrgovişte.[40]

A violent press campaign started against National Peasant Party leadership, more specifically against the Minister of Interior.[41] The pro-communist newspapers requested also aggressively the dismissal of the Bucharest Police Commissioner.[42] Communist leader Teohari Georgescu, under-secretary at the Ministry of the Interior demanded the nomination of the general Vasiliu-Răşcanu a genuine "patriot" as War Minister, and of "a sincere democrat" as Interior Minister.[43] Pro-communist rallies and press energetically claimed the formation of a National Democratic Front government.[44]

Two days after the new Sănătescu cabinet was sworn in, the Soviet Deputy Commissar for Foreign Affairs, A. Vishinsky arrived in Bucharest, on November 8, 1944. His mission was to get the Romanian government's "acceptance" for the payment of the war reparations according to Moscow's conditions and interpretations.[45] Vishinsky had also to deliver to King Mihai a verbal message from the Soviet government "for the purpose of arranging for the better execution of the terms of the armistice".[46] Soon afterwards three new Soviet divisions were brought into the country to be quartered "in industrial areas".[47] The Romanian government transmitted a note to the ACC and inquired whether the troops were destined for a long stay. If yes the fact could be considered as a violation of article III of the Armistice Convention.[48]

Towards the end of November, Soviet authorities informed the Romanian Government that Bucharest police must be reduced to 700 men; Romanian gendarmerie to 14,000 men, and each of the three divisions of the Romanian home army to 3,500 men. In this circumstances, the remaining internal military forces could not effectively maintain the public order.[49]

The political crisis came into open when the traditional parties, the National Peasants and the Liberals decided to withdraw their support from the second Sănătescu cabinet.

Constantin I.C. Brătianu in agreement with Iuliu Maniu considered general Constantin Sănătescu "to be a weak and oscillating prime minister".[50] Brătianu told Burton Berry, the US representative, that the disorders were increasing and the political and economical structure of the country were rapidly deteriorating. The armed communist groups couldn't be disbanded, as promised. The disorders in factories were on the rise. The local legal authorities had been ousted at pistol point in several places by the communists and replaced with men devoted to the NDF. Besides, added the National Liberal leader, the province of Moldavia is virtually isolated from the central government, Romanian administration he been *ejected* from the Northern Transylvania by the Soviet military, and the communication problem became worse.[51]

Understandably most of the grievances expressed against premier Sănătescu were not his fault. As it often happened, in time of major political crisis, somebody was held accountable and that was Sănătescu's case too. He resigned on December 2, 1944.[52]

The public opinion felt increasingly alarmed. On November 28, 1944, Burton Berry, the US representative in Bucharest, informed the Secretary of State that "(C.I.C) Brătianu like most Romanians I have met affirmed that the Soviets planned to take over Romania".[53]

Did A. Vishinsky try to soothe such alarms? At the beginning of the December the Soviet Deputy Commissar for Foreign Affairs talked to professor Mihai Ralea president of the *Socialist-Peasant Party*.[54] "Vishinsky informed Ralea that the Soviet Union does not intend to force a communist regime in Romania and has no desire or plan to incorporate Romania into Soviet Union."

"Since in the past Romania has been hostile and a threat to Russia" added Vishinsky, "*Russia will insist upon enough change in governing classes to guarantee Romania as a genuinely friendly neighbor.*"[55] (my italics D.C.G.) Properly decoded it meant that Moscow did not want a Communist regime in Romania for the time being. The Soviets wanted however "enough change" in the Romanian governing classes. It was an euphemistic way of declaring that the communization of the country was the ultimate target. It is difficult to assess how the Bucharest political circles reacted when privately told about the Vishinsky–Ralea talk.

In fact the communist take over of the Romanian central government was delayed at that time. It will be completed some three months later.

On December 6, 1944, a new coalition cabinet headed by General Nicolae Rădescu was sworn in. The ratio of forces between the traditional parties and the communist NDF remained almost the same. The cabinet will last till February 28, 1945. On March 1, the same A. Vishinsky told King Mihai that Petre Groza is the Soviet choice as premier for the National Democratic Front cabinet. Five days later the communist lead government was in place.

The present volume is the first detailed analysis of the internal Romanian events from December 6, 1944, to March 6, 1945. It is based to a large extent on archival information from the National Archives, Washington DC which include US diplomatic and military reports and Romanian documents as well.

The analysis focuses on the internal Romanian sequence of events as they were perceived and interpreted by the main participants. Special chapters include the debates within the Allied (Soviet) Control Commission on the same developments.[56]

I. THE RĂDESCU CABINET

1. The Formation of the New Cabinet

Prime minister general Nicolae Rădescu and his government were appointed by King Mihai on December 6, 1944. The ratio of forces remained the same between the traditional parties the National Peasants and the Liberals on one side, and the communist lead National Democratic Front (NDF) on the other side.[1] The former had the ministries of Finances, Economy, Agriculture, War Production, Foreign Affairs, Cults and Arts. The NDF was in charge of Justice, Education, Labor, Transportation, Public Work, Social Security, Ethnic Minorities, plus the new office of Deputy Prime Minister.

The communists did not succeed in their attempts to control the Ministry of Internal Affairs and the War Department. The former was taken by premier Rădescu whilst the latter by colonel-general Ion Negulescu.[2]

The second Sănătescu Cabinet, i.e. sworn in on November 6, 1944, was repeatedly blamed by the NDF press of being unable to fulfill the Armistice terms, to operate a purge of "fascists" and to implement reforms. The communists staged ad-hoc meetings and demonstrations.

A week or so after being sworn in, it became quite clear that the government was barely in control.

The Soviet broadcast echoed and backed the NDF attacks against the traditional, pro-Western, parties.

Soviet Vice-Deputy minister for Foreign Affairs, Andrey Vishinsky arrived in Bucharest on November 8, 1944. He avoided any positive talks with the ministers of the coalition government and with the leaders of the traditional parties and spent part of his time with the Romanian communists and their affiliated.[3]

The crisis came into open when the National Peasants and the National Liberals left the Cabinet on December 2, 1944. Rumors of an overt or more likely covert communist coup d'état started running high in Bucharest.

King Mihai entrusted General Nicolae Rădescu with the formation of the new government. The designated premier was a non-party man well known for his moral integrity and democratic stand.

The NDF press raised again the issue of the Interior and War ministries if the NDF were to form a coalition with the "traditional" parties.

On December 4, King Mihai made a bold and authoritative move. He told Vishinsky that the Communist Party's activities may throw the country into anarchy. If this policy continues there is no alternative for the King but to abdicate and leave the country. If the Soviet authorities decide to further back the Romanian communists then the outcome would be the same.

Visibly surprised by the King's statement, Vishinsky denied any Soviet responsibility. He quoted Molotov's declaration of April 2, 1944, with regard to the Soviet non-interference in Romania's interior affairs. The complete fulfillment of the armistice's terms was all that mattered added the Vice Commissar.

Events unfolded rapidly afterwards.

On December 5, General Rădescu told NDF representatives that their bid for the Internal and War ministries was rejected by the National Peasants and by the Liberals. As designated Premier he was contemplating the formation of a non-political government.

All of the sudden, the NDF withdrew its demands and the list of the new cabinet was ready within hours, thanks also to Iuliu Maniu's efforts.[4]

Why the sudden turn? Vishinsky had two effective leverages at his disposal to implement Soviet policies in Romania: the Allied Control Commission and the Communist Party of Romania. How quick and how far would the process go? The answer was pending external and internal developments.

In Athens violent street fighting had spread out between the communist and left wing guerrillas on one side and the anti-communists royalists and republicans backed by British units.[5] Things were on balance and the outcome unclear at the beginning of December. The Churchill-Stalin gentlemen's agreement of October 9, 1944, had given the Soviets 90 per cent predominance in Romania, and the British same percentage in Greece. For the time being however, the arrangement was not confirmed yet by facts so the Soviets presumably adopted a wait and see attitude.

The Soviets probably considered a communist takeover in Romania to be untimely. The withdrawal of traditional parties' ministers from the cabinet and King Mihai's firm attitude would have triggered an open crisis too soon.

At it seems Moscow ordered a temporary stop to the communists' drive to power. A. Vishinsky left Romania unexpectedly on December 8, 1944, canceling previously accepted meetings.

The left wing press dropped its attacks on the traditional parties.[6] Street demonstrations also stopped and even Soviet broadcasts became less hostile against "reactionaries" in Romania.

2. The Program of the Rădescu Government

Premier Rădescu met the press on December 6, 1944, at 12 p.m., after the ministers had been sworn in. He pointed out that his cabinet continues actually the former one. The cardinal point of the program was to strengthen the relations with the USSR: "not to do so would be almost suicidal"; and also fulfill the armistice terms "with all determination".

Order and discipline had to be restored throughout the country. The workers were requested to work hard and continuously and not to take the streets for any claim. Their problems would be approached diligently and attentively by the government. The workers had no right to dismiss at will a factory administration. The wrongdoing managers would be replaced according to the legal provisions.

The forced imposition of the county-prefects and of mayors had to stop. A legal authority could not be superseded by street demonstrations. The preparation had to be speeded up for the local elections.

The printed media was urged to get its information from the government directly, and to stop the press abuses and the misinformation campaigns.

An armistice between the political parties was requested. The armed civil groups had to be dismantled.

The prime minister flatly rejected the rumors that he might favor a dictatorship. He stated: "I hate tyranny, I hate despotism". For fifteen years he had fought any dictatorial attempts. However, he added, "liberty doesn't mean all for one part and none for the other. There should be equal liberty for all".

The pro-communist press stressed one point mainly: Rădescu's promise to strengthen the relations with the USSR. To this goal there was an urgent need to carry on the purge of civil servants and other people of the "former regime"[7].

3. Attempts to Implement the Governmental Program

The control of the local administration was a sensitive issue. The communists had already started to replace forcibly counties' chiefs and mayors of the main towns.[8] The NDF was opposed to free local elections as the communist lead condition was fully aware of its total weakness with the electorate.

A new administration law was enacted. It required a master degree and a minimal age of 25 for nomination as county chief or mayor of important towns. Exceptions were however granted to persons well known for their public activity.[9] Lawyers, engineers, professors, teachers and M.D.'s were appointed.[10]

A statute for national minorities was approved[11] and the corresponding ministry was put in place.[12] The declaration of the nationality was any citizen's free choice. Equality before the law was granted irrespective of the ethnic background.[13] The minority's language could be used in the administration and the judicial procedures whenever the ethnic minority represented at least 30 per cent of the over-all population.[14] Elementary and high schools, and an university would be state sponsored if the required number of minority students was met.[15]

The racial laws were abolished. Some 3,445 reserve officers of Jewish descent were reintegrated within the army.[16] The war time *Jewish Center* was officially dismantled whilst the Federation of the Jewish Communities of Romania got its legal status back.[17]

The problem of war criminals was expressly dealt with by the Armistice Convention.

The prosecution of war criminals and profiteers and the purge of "fascists" from the administration became central to the NDF policies. For years to come "the purge" will be the best tool for the communist lead coalition to get rid of all opponents.

After much bargaining two laws were adopted. Politics intermingled with legal provisions.[18] The National Peasants' and Liberals' representatives succeeded however to maintain some legal judiciary provisions and to defend the principle of the trial based on the law. Special Courts were set up with three professional judges and four members designated by each of the four governmental coalition political parties. The *public prosecutor* was to be selected among magistrates, lawyers or members of other professional organizations thus opening the door to the control of the judiciary by politics. The prosecutor had full power to investigate whilst the Council of Ministers issued the arrest warrants. The latter had precedence over the former when deciding over the defendants to be tried.[19] Politics prevailed again.

The wording of new law was loose enough as to allow a flexible interpretation.

Were accountable for the country's disaster those involved in the political and military alliance with the Third Reich, those who willingly set up the dictatorial regime and helped the nazi propaganda machine, those who gave in Northern Transylvania to be annexed by Hungary in 1940.[20]

The fist three lists of special public prosecutors included some well-known members of the communist party.[21] The government approved a provisional two-months internment of members of the former extreme right wing Iron-Guard.[22] The October 1944 law for the purging of public administration was extended till May 1st 1945.[23]

Meanwhile the communists succeeded in taking over some trade unions as metal workers, printers, journalists, writers. In other places the social democrats came to the forefront under the banner of the *United Workers' Front* agreed upon since September 1944[24] and mostly controlled by the communists.

The provisional trade union committees were "elected" by hand-raising or by administrative pressures, never by secret ballot.

The decree for the Trade Unions expressed the principle of the liberty of organization. Attempts of National Peasant Party to put in place their own unions fell short bitterly opposed by the communists. A General Labor Confederation, i.e. CGM in Romanian acronym, was organized after a Trade Unions' Congress held in Bucharest, on January 26–30, 1945. Its general secretary was the communist leader Gheorghe Apostol. The General Labour Confederation became the Communist Party's springboard for its drive to power.

The leadership of the Trade Unions "*is radical and communist in political complexion*". The syndicates are manipulated "for political purposes" says an US report from Bucharest. During the February 1945 period street demonstrations "the workers appeared in their syndicate groups marshaled and directed by organizers with the National Democratic Front (NDF) bands on their arms".[25]

4. The Soviet Occupation and Its Consequences

A Memo by King Mihai

Romania had lost the war and had to face the consequences. The country was tightly controlled by the Soviets which had full authority within the Allied Control Commission whilst the US and British representatives were relegated to the role of mere observers.

On January 24, 1945, King Mihai sent president Franklin Delano Roosevelt a long memo, in fact, a survey of Soviet policies in Romania. The King expressed his "painful and serious anxiety" as to the country's future "having observed the attitude of various representatives of the USSR in Romania" [26].

a. The military cooperation with the Red Army started on August 24, 1944, when the Romanian Army launched her operations against the Wehrmacht. Till September 20, when the Soviet troops completed their concentration in Transylvania, the Romanian troops carried successfully out two missions:

– the liquidation of all German resistance on Romania territory (56,080 prisoners).

– the necessary cover North and West of the Carpathians range enabling the Soviet units to cross the mountains unhindered and to advance up to 1,000 kilometers within a month.

In a second phase, 14 to 19 Romanian divisions cooperated with the Soviets for the recovery of the Northern Transylvania and the advance into the Hungary and Czechoslovakia.

Despite the massive war effort and the stipulations of the Armistice Convention, the Allied (Soviet) Control Commission imposed a sharp reduction of the Romanian home forces namely: the disbandment of 14 divisions, the demobilization of several other units, a massive decrease of military services and schools, of the frontier guards (by 18 per cent) and of gendarmes (by 20 per cent). The Romanian Navy had been confiscated by the Soviet although there was no mention of it in the Armistice Convention.

Most of the heavy metallurgic industries, of the Army's arsenals, and of the textile and leather industries had worked for the Soviet Army. The Soviet command had taken over some 50 per cent of the sanitary stock of the Romanian Army including all novocaine shots indispensable for any anesthesia. The whole country was a supply-basis for the Soviet troops operating in Hungary and the Balkans. Understandably the Romanian Army waged the war based exclusively on its own supplies. The gallantry and fortitude of the troops had repeatedly been mentioned by the Soviet High Command in its war communiqués.

Thus the Romanian public opinion was hoping that the Three Allies would grant the country the cobeligerence status.[27]

b. The Allied (Soviet) Control Commission denied the Romanian government the reinstatement of the Romanian administration in Northern Transylvania.

True, the ACC acknowledged the retrocession of the Northern Transylvania to Romania as stated by article 19 of the Armistice Convention. Such a provision however "...does not resolve the question of time or way of establishing the Romanian administration..." such a question being connected to the fulfillment of the other important requirements of the Armistice Convention.[28]

The King requested therefore "the immediate reinstallation" of the Romanian administration in the Northern area of Transylvania, i.e. annexed by Hungary through the Vienna "award" of August 30, 1940.

The presence of the Soviet army had prevented the Romanian civil servants to exert their duties in other parts of the country such as Dobrogea with special regards to the Black Sea shore, and Moldavia where no Romanian frontier guard was allowed to control the Romanian-Soviet border.

c. The Allied (Soviet) Control Commission asked orally the Romanian government to send back to the USSR all Romanian refugees from Bessarabia and Northern Bukovina living now in Romania.

The demand was based on the March 8, 1941, decree of the Supreme Soviet, which imposed the Soviet citizenship to all the inhabitants of Bessarabia and Bukovina annexed by the USSR through the ultimatum of June 26, 1940.

The Romanian government's view was that any "repatriation" should be based in the free individual application, as provided by the international standards and laws. This was of no avail and the Soviet authorities pressed for speedy repatriation.[29]

On January 6, 1945, the ACC issued an order to mobilize ethnic Germans[30] aged between 17 and 45 (men) or 18 to 30 (women) and to send them to USSR where there is an acute shortage of labor force. Those avoiding the "mobilization", and persons who might conceal them were facing severe punishments. The Romanian authorities asked with no result to "lessen as much as possible" the consequences of the Soviet order since the deportation of so many persons would hamper the country's economy and fulfillment of the Armistice terms.[31]

d. King Mihai ascertained "with much regret and deep anxiety" the Soviet interference in Romanian domestic affairs, carried out directly or through the Romanian Communist Party.[32] An ad-hoc administration had been imposed in Moldavia. County's chiefs were nominated at Constanţa, Brăila and Galaţi with the direct help of the Soviet army.

A tight censorship had been imposed by ACC to all written and broadcast media, and many radio sets had been confiscated. The independent and opposition press often faced shortage of printing paper and temporary interdiction. The communist press is free to launch vehement attacks on the traditional National Peasant and National Liberal parties, whilst any critique against the left wing parties was promptly sanctioned by ACC censorship.

The Romanian railways system was fully controlled by the Soviets which also taken over the Danubian and high sea commercial fleet, and all harbour installations and facilities.[33]

Last but not the least, came the heavy financial obligations imposed by the Armistice Convention and increased by never ending requirements of the ACC. As a result the notes' circulation soared by 50.4 per cent from 242 to 364 billion lei within less than five months.[34]

King Mihai's *Memoir* never reached President Franklin Delano Roosevelt. Secretary of State Edward Stettinius Jr. considered any official answer as inappropriate. He instructed the US representative at

Bucharest to inform the King that the memo was studied at the State Department.[35]

5. An US Report on Romania

The US Army Chief Military Representative to the Allied (Soviet) Control Commission, general brigadier C.V.R. Schuyler gave a striking image of Romania, after almost six months of Soviet presence. "I believe I have it evident in my cables" wrote general Schuyler in his report of March 25, 1945, "that the Russian hold on the country, economically as well as politically, is now very firm... These is considerable evidence to indicate that the increasing Russian demands may be part of the deliberate plan to break down the nation's economic structure so as to afford an opportunity for rebuilding it strictly along communists lines."[36]

Some figures were significant. The Soviet military authorities required the delivery to the Second Ukrainian Front of the following products: leather foot gear for ladies and children – 40,000 pieces; ladies' tailored suits and gowns – 20,000 pieces; knitted pullover sweaters – 20,000 pieces; ladies' stockings – 30,000 pieces; gentlemen's socks – 30,000 pairs; ladies' linen underwear – 30,000 pairs; gloves – 25,000 pairs; woolen cloth – 30,000 meters; cotton and silk material – 30,000 meters; toilet soap – 200,000 pieces; sugar – 30 tones etc.[37]

The increase in note circulation had been 600 per cent in six months by over 143 billion lei out of which the Soviet demands amounted to 122 billions (about 85 per cent).[38]

There was "a critical shortage" of coal, locomotives, and railroad cars. Of the latter 13,773 had been sent outside of Romania's borders, by January 10, 1945. Unduly burdensome restrictions had been imposed on the use of the railroad transportation for civilian needs with very negative effects on the economy.[39]

The ACC's reacted in a strange way to the very acute shortage of coal. According to the Soviet interpretation, the decline in the domestic output was a deliberate Romanian attempt to sabotage the country's contribution as requested by the Armistice Convention. The ACC ordered an increase of the daily coal extraction to 7,000 tons out of which 4,000 tons had to be delivered to the railways. The order had to be implemented within 24 hours. The ACC approved also imports of coal from Turkey and Bulgaria.[40]

The Romanians viewed the situation differently. In the Prime Minister's letter sent to ACC on February 12, 1945, the decline in the coal output was due to several factors, namely: the deportation to Russia of the miners of German and Hungarian descent; the "repatriation" of the Romanian from Bessarabia and Bukovina; the continued political demonstrations at the coal pits. The Romanian government had already negotiated a daily import of 1,000 to 1,500 tons of Bulgarian coal and a contract with Turkey for a global amount of 175,000 metric tons.[41]

Precise figures are included in brigadier-general C.V.R. Schuyler's report for the deportations. At the ACC's orders, the Romanian government submitted a list of 93,538 ethnic Germans. 80,853 were "mobilized" namely 41,230 men and 38,853 women. Eventually 69,332 were forcibly sent to USSR as "working force".

Additionally 75,336 Romanians from Bessarabia and Northern Bukovina were registered with ACC, between December 20, 1944, and February 1945. Till March 23, 1945, 59,230 persons had been sent back to USSR and 16,106 were still on the "waiting lists".[42]

War reparations to be paid by Romania amounted to $ 300,000,000 (at the 1938 prices), and the protocol signed on January 16, 1945, specified the quantities of products and raw materials to be delivered annually.[43] A special department was organized to secure the restitution of the Soviet goods taken by Romanian authorities from USSR during 1941–1944 war.[44] Severe penalties were instituted by a special decree against any Romanian citizen accountable for "crimes" against "Allied armies" (i.e. Soviet) namely: six months to two years of jail for a kick; one to fifteen years plus fines, for inflicted wounds.[45] Undoubtedly the Minister of Justice who issued the decree felt compelled to strengthen by this way the friendly relations between the Soviet and Romanian individuals.

The internal political truce didn't outlive the end of December 1944 despite the conciliatory attitude of the traditional parties. When the interministerial commission was appointed to settle administrative matters the communists got the best results though traditional Peasant and Liberal parties had the majority. Therefore communist prefects were nominated in the nine most important Moldavian counties vs. three liberals, two national peasants and two non-party prefects. The representatives of the traditional parties expressed however thanks to the communists for their cooperation. The latter didn't keep the previously accepted agreement to appoint as vice-prefects members of the traditional parties wherever a communist prefect was in charge.[46]

Any discussion of preparation for local elections was also postponed. Additionally there was no way to disband the armed communist militia estimated without any proof between 10,000 and 12,000, most of them in Bucharest.[47]

II. THE END OF A THREE WEEKS POLITICAL TRUCE

Hopes for an expanded internal truce faded away with the National Democratic Front's (NDF) appeal to the country on New Year's Day 1945. All charges against the traditional parties, mainly the National Peasants were reiterated. The coalition government (where the communist lead NDF had half of the seats!) was blamed for the delays in the fulfillment of the armistice terms. The NDF requested a speedy land reform, a general purge etc.[1] Ad-hoc statistics claimed that about 32 per cent of the farming land (about 3,000,000 hectares) would be subject to expropriation. (In reality about 1,468,000 hectares were taken from the landlords. 900,000 peasants received about 1,100,000 hectares and remaining land became state property.)

On December 30, 1944, premier Nicolae Rădescu wanted to address the domestic and foreign press correspondents on his government policies. His very cautiously worded text included an implicit appeal to the Soviets and Western Allies to ease their demands with regard to the terms of the Economic Armistice. The alternative would have been the country's famine and ruin. The Soviet Deputy of the Allied Control Commission (ACC), general Vinogradov, ordered the confiscation of the Rădescu's statement, ignoring the latter's explicit protests and threat to resign.[2]

After 42 months of war and with unlimited Soviet requisitions and claims following August 23, 1944, the situation was turning from bad to worse. Cities were for the most part deprived of the minimal needed supplies. The cost of living went up dramatically: 100 in 1939, 1300 on September 1st, 1944, and 2800 – December 25, 1944. The index for fuel and lubricants was 1050 on September 1st, 1944 (as compared to 1939) and 3200 on December 25, 1944.[3]

On the last day of December 1944 the communist leader Gheorghe Gheorghiu Dej arrived in Moscow by a special Soviet railroad car. Dej went in his capacity of Minister of the Transportation and was welcomed by his Soviet counterpart. The news was released in Romania on January 3, 1945.[4] On his return Dej was warmly greeted by communist leaders in Ploiești and Bucharest (January 16).[5] At a press conference a few days later, Gheorghiu Dej stressed the Soviet government's good will and comprehensive attitude in meeting specific Romanian requests in the transportation field.[6] The economic cooperation would have been extended and a trade agreement signed, if it hadn't been for "the questionable and wavering policies carried out by the first government of *the so-called National Democratic Front* and continued by the following cabinets". (my italics D.C.G.) "The feet dragging in the implementation of the armistice conditions" continued the communist leader "has given ground to a distrustfully look on Romania by the Soviet Union". Moreover "antidemocratic activities sponsored by high ranking representatives of the *so-called historical parties*" might explain why the northern part of Transylvania had not yet been reunited with Romania (as specified by the Armistice Convention).[7]

During Gheorghiu Dej's visit to Moscow, the Romanian communist press restarted its editorials and comments against the democratic parties, and especially against Iuliu Maniu and the leaders of the National Peasants Party.[8] The implicit suggestion was that this party should dismiss its present leadership and join the National Democratic Front.

On his return from Moscow, minister Gheorghiu Dej was received by the King. Dej said that he hadn't seen Soviet leaders but "had gained the impression" that a leftist government would be more successful on getting Romania's cobelligerency status, the return of war prisoners, the introduction of Romanian administration in Northern Transylvania, and economic assistance.

Astonishingly the same four points had been previously raised by Romanian Foreign Minister, Constantin Vişoianu at the signing of the Soviet–Romanian protocol on January 16, 1945.[9] At that time general Vinogradov told Constantin Vişoianu that he would cable the topics raised by the Romanian government to Moscow.[10] Now communist minister Dej was stating that these matters could be solved by a leftist cabinet only.[11]

The rumors that spread out were soon confirmed. By January 22 it was known in Bucharest that upon receiving information brought from Moscow by Gheorghiu Dej the communists have decided "to stage a political crisis... within the next few days". The first step would be the public release of the NDF platform calling for the immediate enactment of the land reform law.[12] *Local* Bucharest observers rightly connected the events in Greece to the impending Romanian crisis. It was assumed that "a British decision to back rightist elements in the Balkans" made the Soviet government decide "to back leftist elements in Romania". [13] The assumption was correct only in the sense that Moscow waited for the British to implement their part of the October 1944 Churchill–Stalin agreement for Greece in order to start imposing the Soviet part of the provisions in Romania.

As it seems there was a dissenting voice among the communists. Justice Minister Lucreţiu Pătrăşcanu told Constantin Vişoianu that "he did not favor a crisis now and would work postpone it".[14] There was already some talking of a conflict between the Moscow envoys Ana Pauker and Luca Laszlo, on one hand, and Minister Pătrăşcanu, on the other.[15]

For the traditional political parties, the National Peasants and the Liberals, a coalition government was only way to hamper the communist take over. The public opinion earnestly hoped that once the war is over, the Western powers would be more involved in the Soviet occupied countries.

However the present seemed bleak. The Allied Control Commission (ACC) was tripartite on paper only. The British and US representatives were mere observers and more than once were informed of the Soviet decisions ex-post. Decisions coming from Moscow remained mostly unopposed by the British and US members of the ACC.

The leaders of the traditional parties seemed to be aware of the situation. On November 1st, 1944, Iuliu Maniu had asked* Vice Admiral Stevenson, UK representative to ACC, "if the British intended that Romania be handed over lock stock and barrel to the Russians?" In such a case, he, Maniu was anxious to lead the way, to prepare the country and take it over to communism and thus to the Soviet Union... "If such events were left to the communist party of Romania" – added Maniu's message – "blood would be shed and the only result would be exploitation and unhappiness." [16]

If the Great Britain was opposed to the take over, then "Maniu was prepared to fight communism". He had already drawn the social democrats and Dr. Groza's Ploughmen's Front away from the communist alliance. Thus he was willing to form a majority government including the National Liberals, the Social Democrats and the National Peasants leaving the communists "practically isolated".

Vice Admiral Stevenson assured (Rică) Georgescu that the intention that Maniu anticipated was not held by British government.[17]

As the bad news unfolded any signal from the West gave ground for hope. The Romanian public opinion at large warmly welcomed the British parliamentary statement on Romania's war effort against the Nazi Reich (January 1945).[18]

As the rumors of an impending crisis spread out, political observers in Bucharest were wondering whether the projected communist move meant for them more than an increased gain in power, as it did in October–November 1944.[19]

---

* Through engineer Rică Georgescu, Maniu had asked to meet Vice Admiral Stevenson but was turned down. Therefore Maniu's message was delivered by Rică Georgescu.

Time was running out. The communists were actually determined to oust the traditional parties from the government and seize full control of the central and local administration. Their immediate aim was to placate fears and to get new supporters.

At the railway workers conference, communist minister Gheorghiu Dej surprisingly spoke in favor of entrepreneurs and employees working together for the war effort.[20] The September 1944 program regarding the nationalization of banks and basic industries was postponed.[21] For the time being, on January 26, Dej was reported to have said "the government must be changed".[22] A National Democratic Front manifesto was expected to follow shortly.[23] Justice Minister Lucrețiu Pătrășcanu heading the moderate communist wing was unable to stop the drive if he had ever that in mind. There was some reluctance within the National Democratic Front to follow the renewed communist pressures.[24] Such feelings would very soon be quelled.

III. THE BEGINNING OF A NEW POLITICAL CRISIS

The political manifesto of the communist lead National Democratic Front (NDF) was officially released Sunday January 28, 1945.[1] It targeted known goals such as participation to the United Nations' war effort, integral fulfillment of the Armistice provisions, reintegration of Northern Transylvania, an immediate land reform... The manifesto gave also some clues for basic communist policies, namely: "to gain the confidence and friendship of the United Nations and mainly of the USSR our big neighbour", commercial ties with the democratic countries but especially with the Soviets, support to all "economic factors – industrialists, tradesmen, craftsmen etc., willing to honesty work together for... the development of the economy", purge of all "fascists" from state and private enterprises, severe penalties against saboteurs and profiteers, trials of war criminals, a "democratic" reorganization of the army...[2]

Two words had a special meaning in the NDF manifesto as in any pro-communist literature: "Democracy" – "democratic" and "fascist". "Democratic" or "real democracy" meant any person or development favoring the communist take over. Persons with compromised past were welcomed if they were ready to work unconditionally for the NDF program.

"Fascist" was anyone who opposed the communists irrespective of his former antihitlerist credentials.

The main criteria became one's readiness to obey the emerging new regime.

The manifesto gave green light to a renewed violent vicious campaign against the traditional political establishment. "The reactionary element in the running" circles of the National Peasant and National Liberal parties were considered to have carried out "a policy of duplicity toward the USSR, "through sabotage and procrastination" of the armistice terms, within and outside the government. The "reactionaries" prevented the establishment of sincere and lasting relations with the USSR and other democratic countries; they hampered the introduction of "real democracy" and prevented the country from winning its place "among the peace and liberty loving people".

The manifesto was thus saying that the activity of the National Peasants and Liberals within the government and local administration had so far prevented a complete communist take over.

When asked by press corespondents why a National Democratic Front government was then needed, Gheorghiu Dej asserted that the country's "fundamental problems" couldn't be solved by the existing governments after the August 1944 military coup.[3]

What about the monarchy in Romania? A NDF government, added Gheorghiu Dej, would "loyally cooperate" with His Majesty the King for the "democratization of the country", "the unrelenting fight against fascism", and for "the country's economic renewal".[4] Gheorghiu Dej acknowledged "the important role of His Majesty" in the August 23, 1944 act, and as "constitutional factor". In other words the King was invited to endorse the communist program for the time being.

The main question was how to trigger a major political crisis, to oust the traditional parties and to impose a communist lead cabinet. True, the communists had made important headway during the fall 1944, owing to the direct and/or implicit intervention of the Allied (Soviet) Control Commission. Moreover, a strict Soviet censorship of the media precluded any major criticism against the NDF. Yet the Communist party still shared the power with the National Peasants and the National Liberals within the Rădescu cabinet.

How to go on from this point? How to set off an emergency–explosive situation as to "motivate" the intervention of the Soviet authorities and to bring about a NDF cabinet?

As usual the controlled press launched daily attacks on the "opposition", i.e. the "reactionaries" who were harbouring "fascist elements" throughout the central and local institutions. Editorials relentlessly stressed the need for the NDF government. The repeated pounding of the NDF platform together with the heaviest charges against the opponents labeled as "fascists" was used as a "motivation".[5]

It was also emphasized that a NDF government was almost a precondition to get cobelligerency status for Romania and early return of the war prisoners from USSR. At the same time the good treatment of the prisoners in Soviet camps was detailed in special press reports.[6]

Large street demonstrations followed as a "proof" of mass support for a NDF program. According to the controlled press "almost 300,000 persons" attended a meeting at the University Square in Bucharest and "asked for the NDF government". The real number of participants was a maximum of 34,500 or 11.5 per cent of the total heralded by the communist press.*

---

* The University Square has about 13,800 square meters = 16,507 square yards. With 2.5 persons standing on a square meter the maximum number of participants comes to ca. 34,500.

At the meeting Gheorghe Apostol, secretary of the General Confederation of Labour, condemned the policy "of the reactionary circles led by Maniu". As reported by the controlled press, the participants asked for "immediate arrest" of the war criminals, the fulfillment of the armistice terms, and the enactment of the agrarian reform.[7]

New meetings took place in Bucharest and other places the following days.[8]

The undersecretary for internal affairs communist leader Teohari Georgescu told Romanian press on February 6, 1945, that the purging of fascists from the state administration was proceeding very slowly being sabotaged by influential officials. Georgescu stressed the need of the radical purge of the police imbued with "fascist poison" and added that "reactionary ministers" would not chase a firm policy in this direction.[9]

Then came an incident which was never explained. It was told that "unknown individuals" fired six revolver shots from a car at Miron Constantinescu, chief editor of *Scânteia* the daily of the Communist Party. Did the murder attempt ever take place? No details were released besides the indignant comments of pro-communist papers.

A disobedience campaign was also launched in the rural areas. Guided by communist activists individual peasants started to implement a land reform on their own.[10] Yet for the time being, the overwhelming majority of the countryside did not participate in this forced expropriation.

The National Peasants (NPP) and the Liberals (NLP) made an attempt to release their own platforms. They were stopped short by the communist leader of the Printers' Union. The editorial board of the *Dreptatea*, was asked to stop its criticism of "the working class", of the proposed land reform and the NDF manifesto which provides "genuine solutions" for the country's real democratization. The *Dreptatea* editorial board was thus invited to back unconditionally the communist platform. If it failed to do so *Dreptatea* would not be printed any longer.

There was a different result however. Workers of the Bucharest *Dacia Traiană* printing office wanted the daily to continue.[11] Other printers opposed the leadership of the Printers' Union.

The communist committee reacted promptly and harshly. Four workers – Ion Pungă, Gheorghe Rădoiu, Vasile Marin and Constantin Niculescu – were expelled from the Union and lost their jobs. The alleged reason was "the provocative action" of the four aimed at "breaking apart the unity of the Trade Union".[12] The wording meant any kind of opposition to the dominance and control of the Trade Unions by the Communist Party. The dismissal of the four printers was a clear warning to all workers to avoid or stop opposing the orders.

Premier Rădescu reacted to this new form of censorship. Police and troops were sent to restore the law and the authority of the editorial boards. A delegation of communist printers met the Prime Minister on February 16, and protested against the police and military presence on printing quarters. It is not known how the discussion went on. All one has at disposal in a note published by *Scânteia* saying that the "Prime Minister threatened the delegation that he would take action similar to that taken in Greece. He told workers that he declared war on them, that he would make use of the army and order fire to be open on the workers". The very wording used by *Scânteia*[13] shows a blatant forgery. In a country under strict Soviet control, any talk of that kind would have been a dangerous insanity to any political leader and, for that matter, to anyone at all.

IV. PREMIER RĂDESCU'S FEBRUARY 11, 1945, SPEECH AT THE ARO THEATER

On February 9 caches of arm and ammunitions were discovered. They had been seemingly collected with the approval of Petre Groza the Vice President of the Council of Ministers and of General Stănescu, under-secretary to the Interior Ministry. The arms were to be used in a possible coup d'état for the NDF government.

Premier Nicolae Rădescu summoned communist, social democrat and trade unions representatives and indignantly demanded the immediate resignation of the officials involved. The representatives protested their serious desire for the continuation of the governmental coalition. They convinced the Prime Minister to agree to the formula of "unlimited vacation" for Petre Groza and a "sick leave" for General Stănescu.[1] General Rădescu decided a cabinet reshuffle aimed at eliminating Dr. Petre Groza's Ploughmen Front and replacing some National Peasant ministers with other people from the same party. The leader of the NPP was called to Bucharest for consultations.[2]

Prior to any move, Premier Rădescu decided to inform the country. His speech was planned to be delivered at Bucharest Theater *Scala* on Sunday February 11, 1945. The previous night, National Democratic Front members packed the hall and all entrances ready to boo the Prime Minister. Hearing that Rădescu moved to the near by Theater Aro where his broadcasted speech was met with repeated approvals and cheers. The Printers' Union refused to print the speech. Nevertheless the country was informed through the radio.

Rădescu told the audience that being a non-party man and a dedicated democrat, with no intention of carrying on polemics with anyone, he would like to inform the country of the situation and ask of his opinion on the government. He listed the three major goals of his administration as: the continuation of war to the final defeat of hitlerism, a loyal fulfillment of the armistice terms, and the maintenance of order as a prerequisite to any productive work. There are however people who constantly try to discredit all efforts. These people like a state of chaos, see bad in all what is done, bring absurd changes labeling many officials as fascists and hitlerists and waging poisonous campaign of slanders. Rădescu asked that this "harmful system of political conflict" be brought to an end, and protested against the charges directed against members of his cabinet.

The Prime Minister insisted on everyone's right "to express one's thoughts in writing..". He continued: "one part of the press adopts a tone of rare violence and a bearing which is not of a nature to increase the prestige of the press as institution, whose role is of paramount importance in the education of the people".[3] Moreover printers saw fit to take upon themselves the censorship of some newspapers. They refused to print certain statements and in one case decided the suspension of a paper.[4] Do the workers have the right "to suppress the principal attribute of democracy – liberty?" "What, then is dictatorship and nazism" asked Rădescu. "What difference is between what was done under the Antonescu regime[5] when everything was written to order and what the workers are doing now?"

As for the Trade Unions, they should be truly "trade and professional" and less political. "Political adventures" should come to an end and everyone should rise against agitation. As for the land reform law it has to be enacted as soon as the war ends. Any earlier implementation would bring much social and economic confusion.[6] The Prime Minister also referred to the co-belligerence and Northern Transylvania.

The audience repeatedly met Rădescu's speech with slogans such as: "We want Liberty", "Long Live Liberty", "The King and the Country". His last sentence was followed by "an enthusiastic demonstration for the sovereign" and the audience sang the national anthem. On February 12 at 1 p.m., the Prime Minister made a second broadcast in order to explain what happened a day earlier. He added that printers had received orders from their union to avoid printing any information with regard to the meeting of the previous day, except for the communist version of the events. Rădescu ended with an appeal to all the workers: "...I ask one thing for your own good and for that of the country: do not be led astray by others to become their tools but attend to your work which is now of paramount importance." Astonishingly, some papers reproduced the second Rădescu broadcast.[7]

This development provided the communists with a new opportunity to escalate the political crisis. The headlines of the pro-communist press read: "The Sunday's hooliganic demonstration. Ilie Lazăr, Comaniciu and Fărcăşanu leading gangs of the Iron–Guardists and fascists".[8] The citizens waiting at the Scala Theater since dawn became indignant when General Rădescu spoke from another hall – wrote left wing newspapers. General Rădescu's disdain toward the people pushed him to broadcast from another place, said the communist Justice Minister Lucreţiu Pătrăşcanu. Gheorghe Apostol, the communist general secretary of the recently organized Trade Unions urged the audience to strike with all might those who try to stop the genuine democratization of the country.[9] Apostol added: Rădescu made his speech at the *ARO* Theater surrounded by police officers, gendarmes, army addressing an audience of Iron-Guardists disguised into young National Peasants and Liberals. Scuffles irrupted on the streets in the area between the "hooligans" and "peaceful

National Democratic Front supporters". The same "hooligans "and "fascists" went to the royal palace square shouting "Rădescu the order" and aggressed "isolated groups of citizens supporters to be NDF sympathizers". Afterwards some 500 "reactionaries" went to the Scânteia Publishing House and set on fire some copies of the communist daily.[10]

Thus the rewriting of the History started the very days when the events were unfolding.

The communist leadership seized the opportunity to further increase the political tension. The Trade Union mobilized people at the Nation Square (Piaţa Naţiunii) on Tuesday February 13, 1945. "In response to the fascist gangs half a million people have demonstrated for democracy and liberty, for the agrarian reform, for the NDF government" – such titles read the headlines of the pro-communist official version.

In February 1945, the capital had around one million inhabitants. One wonders how it was possible to cram 500,000 persons into a plaza large for ca. 50,000?

The US military representative to the Allied (Soviet) Control Commission in Bucharest cabled next day that the demonstration "was attended by approximately 25,000 people. After the meeting they paraded down Calea Victoriei to King's Palace and dispersed without disorder". [11]

Eleven slogans were repeatedly shouted by participants, demanding the arrest of some National Peasants leaders and of the "fascists". One slogan only called for an "immediate" land reform, and another one hailed the printers as "the defenders of democracy".

The main speaker, communist leader Gheorghe Gheorghiu Dej accused the "reactionary elements" at the ARO Theater of the "hostile actions" planned long ago against the "whole people", against "all democrats" and "good-Romanians". The reactionaries showed their hostility even toward "our big allies, foremost toward the Soviet Union".[12] Dej urged the peasants to implement the land reform themselves, irrespective of law procedures. "Citizens" – added the communist minister – "do not hesitate when meeting these rabid dogs. Wherever you meet them, hit them firmly, crush them, expose anyone who would cover up those hitlerist thugs." The crowds shouted "down with fascists, death to the fascists". A protest–motion "voted" by the popular assembly condemned the meeting at the ARO Theater, the "fascist gangs" operating under "the cover of the reactionary leadership of the so-called historic parties". The participants demanded a NDF government and regime of "genuine democracy".[13]

The pro-communist press announced street demonstrations in many cities throughout the country such as: Ploieşti, Moreni, Tîrgovişte etc.[14]

Attacks were also directed against the National Peasant members of the cabinet. Agriculture Minister Ion Hudiță was accused of sabotaging "the spring sowing campaign". In reality, professor Hudiță became a political target because he opposed the communist take over of the Ministry of Agriculture.[15] The representatives of the NDF withdrew from the governmental commission for the land reform. The alleged explanation on the withdrawal was that Rădescu's government seemed unable to implement the land reform.[16]

The real issue was political competition. The National Peasants' project was a more radical one leaving 30 hectares only (74,100 acres) to the landlord. The communists favored a 50 hectares ceiling per estate. Thus the National Peasants' project offered more land for expropriation despite communist allegations against the platforms of the traditional political parties. There were however major differences between the two projects. The National Peasants considered private property and individual rights and liberties as the very foundation of social and economic structures. The communists' program was a tactical move towards their real goal, the rural collectivization and the dictatorship of the proletariat.

Polemics were also targeted against Aurel Leucuția the National Peasant Minister of the Economy.[17] The communist undersecretary for internal affairs Teohari Georgescu resigned from the "purge commission" in protest against the scuffles in Bucharest on Sunday, February 11, 1945: "incompatible with a democratic regime" and also because "the fascist reactionary elements" were still present in the police force.

The activity of the cabinet was virtually blocked whereas the street demonstrations and the agitation within the factories continued.

New pressures were added to the opposition papers. Since the Printers Union refused to print Rădescu's speech, *Viitorul* the daily of the National Liberal Party was published by volunteers in one sheet edition, which started Tuesday, February 13. The next day the editor of *Viitorul* fired the local union employees who refused to print the paper. On Saturday February 17 *Viitorul* was suppressed by the Soviet authorities through the Allied Control Commission (ACC) for publishing material contrary to the terms of the Armistice Convention.[18]

The incriminated text was a postcard sent by a peasant from the Iași district to the leader of the Liberal Party. The Soviet censor claimed that the postcard included a ciphered message. Romanian investigation proved that this was not true but the ACC maintained its allegations.[19] Almost concomitantly, an editorial of the pro-communist *România Liberă* requested a "severe control of the printed media" and "a serious purge" among the newsmen.[20]

Clearly disturbed by recent developments, Romania's Minister for Foreign Affairs Constantin Vişoianu informed the US political representative in Bucharest that as regards the press "the situation today is far worse than during Antonescu regime" and that "the Soviet authorities are mixing directly in Romanian affairs and this is leading directly to the destruction of the state".[21]

General Nicolae Rădescu was fully aware that the situation was getting out of hand. On Monday, February 19 he informed the same US representative of the four recent developments: 1) by order of the NDF undersecretary of agriculture, NDF activists had started distributing land to the peasants in the Constanţa and Botoşani counties; 2) on the weekend NDF groups except for the social democrats had attempted to seize the county administration in Craiova and Turnu Măgurele; 3) Rădescu had unsuccessfully tried to dismiss vice-premier Petre Groza at the Saturday February 18 cabinet meeting, and 4) by order of the Allied (Soviet) Control Commission all Romanian tanks including five old ones guarding the Royal Palace would have to be removed from Bucharest.[22]

The Prime Minister reacted promptly. By royal decree the three undersecretaries for internal affairs were dismissed, among them the influential communist leader Teohari Georgescu. Though his office had been abolished by legal decree, the communist undersecretary refused to leave the building and sent a telegram to all county chiefs (prefects) that they should continue to receive his instructions and not take into consideration Rădescu's orders.[23] "I advise you most emphatically not to execute orders directed against the people given by General Rădescu who has proved by his dictatorial actions to be enemy of the people."[24]

When NDF remonstrators stormed a county administrative building and imposed a new prefect, three companies of gendarmes, some 700 men, restored the legal authority and temporarily arrested the leaders of the NDF attack.

Two closely related new developments brought the staged crisis between the General Rădescu and the NDF to a high point.

V. THE INCIDENTS AT THE MALAXA FACTORY

On Tuesday February 20, special editions of *România Liberă* and *Scânteia* announced that the head of the General Labour Confederation Mr. Gheorghe Apostol had been "shot by the fascists" at the *Nicolae Malaxa* factory in Bucharest. "A compact group of Iron-Guardists armed with machine guns, automatic weapons and pistols, added the newspapers, entered the plant and barricaded inside." At 10:30 a.m. they opened the fire on the delegates of the Trade Unions. Gheorghe Apostol seriously wounded was rushed to the hospital. Workers backed by "citizens patriots" surrounded and disarmed the fascists. The report concluded: "Today's extremely serious events are a follow up of general Rădescu's speech at ARO and the subsequent hooligan and fascist disorders. General Rădescu has to resign since this is the people's willingness. His resignation would also fit within the declaration of the Crimean Conference."[1] A more elaborated version of the events was released by the pro-communist media the next day. According to it a group of the Iron-Guardists headed by Mărculescu, engineer Constantinescu Gherca and "others" wanted to change the existing union committee of the factory forcibly and by surprise. They proceeded to a sham vote using precasted ballots, on Monday February, 19, 1945. Two groups of gendarmes commanded by major Diaconu arrived at the factory whilst captain Iorgu Popescu of the Military Justice sealed the ballot box. The next day (February 20), the Iron-Guardists continued their "provocation" and eventually sequestrated the factory's union committee locking its members in the big Conference Hall. At 8:10 a.m. Gheorghe Apostol with V. Brătfăleanu and Emil Angheliu from the Executive Committee of the General Labour Confederation requested permission to enter the Malaxa courtyard. They were stopped at the gate by some Iron-Guardists shouting "we do not recognize any General Confederation of Labour!". Meanwhile railway workers arrived at the Malaxa Factory to help their comrades molested by the "fascists". Gheorghe Apostol's group including railway workers succeeded eventually to enter the courtyard (by interrupting the electric power and thus opening the gate). They went to the general management building where they set free the members of the committee who had been locked in the conference hall. At the same time "several hundreds fascists" armed with sticks and stones and shouting "Rădescu and Order" were advancing toward the general management building. Facing the impeding danger the Apostol group started to retreat. As they approached gate no. 2 shots were fired and Gheorghe Apostol was hit in the stomach by a bullet, being rushed to the Elias Hospital. In the meantime new railway workers came to rescue and disarmed the "fascist gangs". "Weapons of all kinds and calibers, automatic weapons, machine guns, iron bars etc. were seized." Around one hundred persons were detained and interrogated. During the events one Malaxa worker was killed and nine others injured.[2] The comments of the pro-communist newspapers blamed bitterly Iuliu Maniu, the "reactionaries" of the National Peasant Party, and general Rădescu for the outcome of the Malaxa incidents. Ad-hoc meetings were held by the Trade Unions demanding that perpetrators be punished and the premier dismissed.

According to a statement of the National Democratic Front Council, "*Romania is thrown into the civil war by the word and deed of the general Rădescu, of Iuliu Maniu* and of all those who directly of indirectly arm and back the still very active fascist and ironguardists elements".(my italics D.C.G.). The statement considered the dismissal of the three undersecretaries for internal affairs as illegal, as a dictatorial, anti constitutional and antidemocratic act of the prime minister. General Rădescu was blamed for being the rallying center of all "reactionary and fascist groups" and therefore had to go. The National Democratic Front stated its readiness to assume full governmental responsibility in order to put Romania on a solid track for a free and "democratic" development. All that was in accordance with "the spirit of Crimean declarations".[3]

The local committee of the Bucharest trade unions backed the communist version of the events at once. The manifesto claimed that "the reaction headed by prime minister Rădescu and Maniu had begun the attack on the democratic forces", that "the legionaries and the fascists terrorized the Malaxa workers" and that "the criminal attack of gangs of murderers was the result of the six months of reactionary government".[4]

The aim was to blow the Malaxa incidents out of proportion, to claim that democracy is in jeopardy and to present a NDF government as the sole solution to the crisis.

What actually happened at the Nicolae Malaxa factory?

The National Peasant *Dreptatea* gave a totally different sequence of events. The workers of the factory were dissatisfied with "the abuse and dishonesty" of the self-appointed NDF committee lead by Vasile Mauriciu. They demanded the election of a new union committee. The day of the election, Monday February 19, the representative of the workers Mr. Mărculescu was severely beaten by Mr. Mauriciu and his men. Mr. Mărculescu was saved by "indignant workers", and the ballot took place with the following results: about 4,500 votes for a new independent committee, about 700 votes for the communist lead committee.

Meanwhile "authorized representatives of the factory" searched Mr. Mauriciu's house (member of NDF) where they discovered a revolver, 500,000 lei and two tickets for horse races worth of 200,000 lei.

After the vote, the General Assembly of the Workers formulated the following demands: 1. The vote for the factory committee to be held under the supervision of a civil or military magistrate.[5] 2. The immediate release of the workers arbitrarily detained by NDF groups[6] and 3. The dismissal of engineer Korcinsky who took over the management of the factory without the workers' consent.

On Tuesday, February 20, trucks with workers from the railway and from the municipal gas, electricity and water works drove up to the gates of the N. Malaxa factory, to help the ousted Mr Mauriciu. Pro-communist and non-communist workers scuffled.

Those who arrived from outside opened fire on the Malaxa workers and one bullet hit also Mr. Gh. Apostol. *România Liberă* reported that Dragu Stan, locksmith at the factory, was killed. The daily *Dreptatea* specified that Dragu Stan was a member of the National Peasant Party! [7]

Comparing the two versions, the *Dreptatea* sequence of events has more consistency and is more explicit than the *România Liberă* report. A clear picture of the incidents would need more details. Even so, the communist tactics came into open: a) the blame for the incident was immediately thrown on general Rădescu and the leadership of the National Peasant Party; b) the whole development was blown out of proportion and denounced as an impending civil war prepared at length by "fascist and reactionary elements"; c) the Rădescu government must go and be replaced by the NDF administration.

Who fired the shots? To my knowledge an official judiciary report on the Malaxa plant incident has never been publicly released. The communist media did not go into details beyond its printed version. A report prepared by the US military representative and the Allied (Soviet) Control Commission for Romania confirms the main facts. An attempt to hold union elections was made on Monday February 19. The next day when it appeared that left-wing elements at the plant would be defeated, a group of several hundreds armed workers appeared from adjoining industrial establishments, and demonstrated in front of the plant. When they attempted to enter shots were exchanged with workers inside the plant who had also possessed themselves arms. During the course of the melee labor leader Apostol was seriously wounded.[8]

What happened to the about one hundred people who were detained? At the mid March, 42 workers from the Malaxa plant and 18 printers of the daily *Dreptatea* were still in custody of the Bucharest Police Headquarters. No charges were filed in the police register but a note indicated that they were held upon the order of the Minister of the Interior, Communist Party leader Teohari Georgescu. Two printers from *Dreptatea* interviewed by Western members of the Allied Control Commission showed evidence of physical abuse. They confirmed their arrest and imprisonment by NDF civilians and that all detainees were submitted to continuous maltreatment.[9]

VI. A SPECIAL PARTNER TO THE COMMUNIST TAKEOVER: THE SOVIETS. PREPARATIONS FOR THE LAST DRIVE TO POWER

In the wake of the Malaxa plant incidents the communists called for a protest mass meeting on Saturday, February 24 at 2 p.m. in the Piaţa Naţiunii (Nation's Plaza). Inciting handbills were distributed throughout the town. Their wording was most vicious: "General Rădescu, Iuliu Maniu, Ilie Lazăr, in collusion with the fascist remnants, are driving our country to a new disaster. The enemies of the people wish to install a dictatorship on the model of the disastrous and bloody regime of the executioner Antonescu". The NDF called to all "young and old, town dwellers and peasants, men and women of all social categories, civilians and army men" to demonstrate against "the treacherous clique", for the NDF government: "Down with Rădescu! Death to the Fascists!"[1] On February 23 new handbills were distributed. "The United Workers' Front" exhorted its members to "respond with ten blows to one blow of the fascists".[2] On the same day the official communist newspaper *Scânteia* printed the NDF appeals to the women and to the "officers, non-commissioned officers and other ranks!": Iuliu Maniu, General Rădescu "and others around them" are trying to use the army "for their criminal plans and for the oppression of the Romanian people". The same reactionaries ordered fascists to open fire on the workers' leaders and sent "officers and soldiers to sabotage the war production" in the factories. The same "deadly enemies" of the people were using army units "to defend the estates of the great landowners" and were "driving the country to civil war". The army who was promised a better pay and living standards, was thus requested to disobey orders issued by Rădescu, to join NDF demonstration and to ensure "a reliable rear zone" for the Front.[3] King Mihai was not mentioned at all despite the fact that the army was truly devoted to the monarchy at that time.

The NDF council told the "women, mothers, and wives" that the same Rădescu government was supporting "shameless profiteering" with prices soaring even higher, was spreading out hatred and disunion, was instigating "children against parents" and "brothers against each other", and maintained that women's "only place is in the kitchen". The NDF Council urged the women to join a National Democratic Front government which would extirpate the profiteering, ensure the return of the war prisoners from the USSR, and guarantee equal rights for men and women.[4]

In separate statements the Social Democrats[5] and the Ploughmen's Front[6] expressed directly or indirectly their allegiance to the communist lead NDF.

On 27th anniversary of the Red Army, the NDF Council sent a telegram to "the man of genius leading the liberating army, Marshal Stalin" and pledged to fight with all "its strength" for the destruction of "fascist remnants" in Romania, "for the sincere application of the magnanimous armistice and the historic decisions of the Crimea Conference, for Romania's eternal friendship with the Soviet Union".[7]

The pro-communist media launched an all-out propaganda war. According to the editorial of *România Liberă* of February 25, 1945, "Rădescu and Maniu were planning civil war;"[8] Maniu and Rădescu "have made it their aim to provoke bloody incidents which might be transformed by repetition and aggravation into a sort of civil war". The government includes "the country worst enemies" and "threatens to repeat the slaughter of the past through military terror". Moreover this "most reactionary clique" decided "to direct provocation against the state authority" and to push "to street fighting". This "reactionary clique" decided to reorganize a parallel meeting "on the same day, at the same hour and almost in the same place as the NDF". By planning this Maniu "deliberately aims at the bloody street fighting of civil war".[9]

This last phase for the imposition of a NDF government highlights the communist procedure based on the invention and the rewriting of history.

The first step was the distortion, misinterpretation and even the invention of facts. Second came a media barrage aimed to project the communist version of events. Concomitantly, anyone's attempt to speak out the truth, to explain what really happened was stopped from the very beginning.

Year after year the *official version* continued by repetition and insertion into editorials, comments, articles, and text books. As time went by, the number of persons who might had witnessed the contrary diminished and public opinion at large assimilated the asserted facts.

Yet there were other specific circumstances. In February 1945 there was more. There was a special partner whose presence was instrumental to the communist take over and to its invented sequence of events.

The special partner was the Soviet government and its army.

On February 22, 1945, *Pravda* took the offensive with the lengthy account of the Romanian developments. The story was identical to that of the Romanian communist press. Yet *Pravda* came with some new points, interpretations and assertions such as: the NDF program of January 28, 1945, "was unanimously approved by the mass of the population". Teohari Georgescu's accusations that the Rădescu government was "sheltering reactionary elements" was backed by a "considerable part of the Romanian press". Rădescu's speech of February 11, was "entirely directed against the democratic elements" and increased the tension. The Prime Minister had urged the workers to be less involved in politics on more in their work: "keeping the workers out of the public life is typical of a fascist regime", added *Pravda*. Rădescu's refusal to implement immediately the agrarian reform and his proposal to postpone it to the end of the war is similar to the promises made after World War I, when the agrarian reform was to be carried out "at an opportune moment, but this moment never came" and the Romanian peasants were bitterly deceived.* The scuffles in front of the ARO Theater after Rădescu's speech on February 11, were considered by *Pravda* "barbarous maltreatment of the demonstrators by the fascists". The police "supported the hooligans and bandits". The Printers' Union was right when it refused to print the daily *Dreptatea* which "hurled at the NDF... the dirtiest and most libelous accusations". "There is freedom of the press" added the editorial "but not for hitlerist and their agents!" Last but not least, "a provocative aggression against the factory committee was arranged" by hitlerist elements at the Malaxa plant on February 20, 1945. To sum up, the Rădescu government had no popular support and was unable to set up a strong state order in Romania.

The *Pravda* article ended with the warning that "Soviet opinion cannot look unmoved the internal struggle between democratic and fascist elements in Romania. *This is not solely an internal Romanian affair.* (my italics D.C.G.). The war is not yet over... We (the Soviets) cannot forget for the moment that Romania is behind the lines of the Red Army front, and that the domination of the pro-fascist elements must be liquidated in the rear of this front. This is also a requirement of the historic decisions of the Crimea Conference".[10]

Pravda's intervention had a twofold aim.

On the one hand it credited the local communist version of the events and offered the standardized account of an invented history. On the other hand it stressed that the Romanian developments could became threaten-

---

* *Pravda* did not mention the 1921 land reform when 6,125,000 hectares were expropriated from the landowners and distributed to the peasants. It was the largest land reform ever made in Romania's history and was preceded by the 1864 rural law when 2,038,640 hectares were divided among 511,896 peasant families. Thus the 1864 and 1921 reforms transferred in all 8,163,640 hectares to the peasantry. The communist land reform of March 1945, gave 1,100,000 hectares to cca. 900,000 families.

ing since the Red Army needed a safe rear front area (in February 1945 the front line was al least 650 km westward of Bucharest).

There was a prompt follow up by *Graiul Nou* (The New Word), the official newspaper of the Soviet Army in Romania. Its editorial "Order should reign in the rear lines of the Red Army"[11] was meant to tell the Romanians and the Western allies that the Soviet army's views were identical to *Pravda*'s.

Yet irrespective of the statements of the controlled press, the confrontations with the "fascists" was a mere pretext. At stake was the communist take over of the central and local administration. A minority guided by party activists had taken the streets and was portrayed by a vociferous left-wing press as expressing people's will. The demonstrators did not exceed 50,000, i.e. 5.5 per cent of the Bucharest population. The communists knew all too well that free elections would prove the overwhelming weakness of the National Democratic Front. The only way to seize complete power was to disrupt and eventually overthrow the country's legal authority and to replace it by self-appointed communists or their affiliates. All that was needed was a make believe sequence of events on which the invented history could be written and imposed to everyone. This was the possible since the whole country was tightly controlled by the Soviet Army and commissars.

The last act started on Sunday February 24, 1945.

Reactions of the National Peasant Party

In the beginning the National Peasant Party adopted a wait and see attitude toward the new premier Nicolae Rădescu. The president of the National Peasant Party (NPP) was known by his opponents as being "the perfect oppositionist". Iuliu Maniu possibly viewed the Rădescu government as short lived. The NPP leader wished therefore to be fully prepared for the next phase of the confrontation with the communists. As it seems the Prime Minister was initially puzzled by Maniu's opposition tactics.

After Rădescu's memorable speech of February 11, the attitude of NPP changed. Iuliu Maniu told his associates that although General Rădescu had talked very sincerely, yet politically the situation in Romania was not ripe for such a direct approach at this time. Maniu also considered that the Prime Minister had made a political error by opposing immediately agrarian reform. However taking into account the slander attacks and the virulent campaign for the NDF government, the National Peasants felt it their duty to stay united with the National Liberals behind the prime minister. Iuliu Maniu did not attempt to hold NPP counter-demonstrations throughout the country. On February 22, *Dreptatea*'s editorial was an uncompromising exposure of the communists' goals as compared to the National Peasants guide lines: the latter included full freedom of writing within the legal frame, the distribution of land to the peasants with due respect to the law and the rules imposed by circumstances, a legal administration established by and originated in the authority of the state, the constructive work to increase the production, the punishment of all responsible for the war.

The communists, reminded *Dreptatea* advocated for: a "freedom" of a controlled press, distribution of the land by lawless confiscation of the property, an administration arbitrarily chosen and forcibly imposed by NDF people. The communists agree in theory to increase the output but in fact they order frequent interruptions for street demonstrations. They shout about death to the fascists but the only those who have not joined the NDF ranks.

"All orderly elements" added the *Dreptatea* editorial "do not and never will understand that the time of dictatorship which ruled a country and ruined a people may be revived in any form by anyone". *Dreptatea* concluded: "hypocrisy, bad faith, lies, slander, libel are not creative elements. They are characteristic of autocratic, unwanted, dictatorial governments. They do not suit us. And the National Peasant Party will fight them with utmost energy as in the past". It was the first time since August 1944 that the communists were openly told their deeds.

The next day, handbills were distributed on Bucharest streets calling "all Romanians" to attend a National Peasant meeting, at the Royal Palace Square, on February 24, at 1:00 p.m. Another handbill announced the students that "Iuliu Maniu will speak in reply to those who distort the truth".[12]

The planned meeting seemed to be a reversal of the former NPP decision not to organize rallies under the circumstances. Or was it rather a political maneuver as it was considered by "reputable" Bucharest sources?[13]

One day before the demonstration, the NDF press gave large coverage to a "democratic group of the National Peasant Party" which issued an appeal to members of their party. In a wording similar to the *Scânteia* articles the NPP dissidents alleged that the actual National Peasant leaders had financed "from the secret funds" the Iron-Guard movement; that during the war they hoped for a conflict between the great allies and therefore "stubbornly refused to get into direct touch with the USSR;" they avoided to form a political government for the armistice as "desired" by the allies[14]; they received Iron-Guardists into their party's ranks (similarly the communist party admitted Iron-Guardists into its ranks); that after

August 1944 they continued "their vicious fight against the introduction of a real democracy" thus "opening the gates to a catastrophic civil war". For all the above mentioned reasons the eleven persons who signed the appeal decided to form the democratic branch of the NPP. This new party agreed with "the NDF minimal program of government" but stressed it would maintain its independence, its program and its emblem.[15] No prominent leader of the NPP signed the appeal. Its initiator was Anton Alexandrescu, allegedly former secretary general of the National Peasants Youth. *The Democratic NPP* remained an insignificant member of the National Democratic Front and almost disappeared from politics after November 1946 elections.

VII. SATURDAY, FEBRUARY 24, 1945

In the morning of Saturday February 24, 1945, one more salvo of huge propaganda barrage was fired by the official communist daily, *Scânteia*. All citizens were summoned to the Nation's Plaza (Piața Națiunii), that very day, at 2 p.m.: "Workers, peasants, officers, non-commissioned officers, soldiers, employees... women, old and young[1]... your rights and your freedom are at stake."[2]

The meeting started, as announced. The plaza was packed with people, trade unionists mainly, also onlookers. How many? "Over 600,000* claimed the pro-communist press,[3] i.e. at least 60 per cent of Bucharest's population. According to US observers there were 50,000 at loose estimation.[4] A resolution was presented and "unanimously approved". The NDF condemned "with profound indignation" the action of Maniu and Rădescu "in encouraging and protecting the fascist terrorists bands of Hitler's agents", also in giving support to profiteers and their price rises. The meeting asked for enactment of the land reform, for "the immediate stabilization of prices and the increase of wages", for the purge of all fascists, for the introduction of "real democracy"...[5] Then, the demonstrators marched to the Royal Palace Square with flags, written slogans and the portraits of Stalin, Roosevelt, Churchill and King Mihai.

What happened next?

According to the communist version, as the participants advanced in Calea Victoriei, shots were fired from the National Theater building[6], then rounds of other shots started from the Ministry of Interior followed by others from the Royal Palace. "Most of the rounds were fired into the air, some were aimed at the population." After a few moments of panic the indignant crowd stood firm shouting "Down with Rădescu the Murderer"! Shots were also fired on the whole Victoria street from the Bucharest prefecture to the Athenee Palace and from other isolated locations. Communist leaders took the floor on an improvised platform.[7] The leitmotif was "we have been provoked, we demonstrated peacefully and have been fired at, Rădescu the criminal must go!" All speakers told the participants to leave the Palace Square and to wait for new orders.

---

* At least ten layers of superposed persons were needed to get the 600,000 in the Nation's Plaza. Bucharest had ca. 1,000,000 inhabitants at the beginning of 1945!

What happened actually? Three inquiries by Romanian military magistrates and two reports by US observers offer many specifics and details.

On February 24, at 10:30 a.m., colonel Rădulescu, commander of the Special Gendarmes battalion was instructed by lieutenant magistrate Florin Olteanu, Military Examining Prosecutor to the Court Martial of the Military Command of Bucharest, on how to proceed in case of disturbances. Colonel Rădulescu was told that his soldiers should not fire on the demonstrators, whatever they did, without lieutenant Florin Olteanu being present. Olteanu in his turn was instructed to get in touch with the NDF delegates, if incidents occur. The Military Command of Bucharest also issued orders stating clearly that shots should be fired in the air only after legal warning, in order to avert incidents. Would the demonstrators try to forcibly enter the Ministry of the Interior, the procedure had to be followed according to the regulation of the garrison on duty.[8]

Towards 16:40 hrs (4:30 p.m.) columns of demonstrators started to enter the Royal Palace Square coming orderly from downtown Calea Victoriei. They were preceded by other crowds which had entered the square some fifteen minutes earlier. There was skirmish and some confusion around the statue of King Carol I, but calm was restored after a short while.

The columns of demonstrators took up their places in groups starting from Athenee Palace hotel in the northern part of the Palace Square to the southern part. By 5:30 p.m. the whole plaza in front of the main entrance of the Ministry of the Interior was packed.[9]

A second minor incident occurred towards 5 p.m. Several cars with armed soldiers under the command of a captain arrived close to the Ministry of the Interior coming from Strada Academiei. Many demonstrators were waiting for the meeting to start. Seeing the cars the participants started to shout. Then lieutenant colonel magistrate Oreste Dobrotescu got off one car asking the crowd to withdraw from the front of the Ministry. Some from the throng replied: "Long Live Military Justice, come to see the justice done, as the army had come to murder us, who have come unarmed..."[10]

Lieutenant colonel Dobrotescu explained that the troops would not intervene unless the crowd refused to return to their homes in order. Some demonstrators began to withdraw. Lieutenant colonel Dobrotescu told the captain in command to keep the troops inside the cars as to avoid further shouting. Then lieutenant colonel Dobrotescu entered the Ministry of Interior. There he met the Prime Minister and received general Oncică's call with the order to send the cars with troops back to the military command.

Outside, lieutenant colonel Dobrotescu found a new uproar. A major of a frontier guard regiment had ordered the captain in command to get the troops out of the cars. Lieutenant colonel Dobrotescu requested that communist leader Gheorghiu Dej (who was there) disperse the demonstrators in order to avert a confrontation. A Soviet officer arrived at that moment and agreed with Dobrotescu's viewpoint. The Soviet officer asked the frontier regiment major to send the troops back to the cars. That was done and the uproar died down as soon as the cars left for the military command headquarters.[11]

The bloody incidents started short after 5:30 p.m. As the last demonstrators entered the Royal Palace Square from downtown Calea Victoriei, the first automatic pistol shots were fired from "Ilfov" apartment building opposite the Ministry for the Interior.[12] People began to run away assuming that the troops had fired, some demonstrators also fired shots at the building of the Ministry of Interior. Some bullets went through the windows into the Prime Minister's and a former undersecretary's offices.[13]

In the uproar, some demonstrators crowded on Wilson street (today Dem.I. Dobrescu) and tried to forcibly enter the building of the Ministry of Interior through a back gate. The soldiers fired a volley of shots in the air and succeeded in driving the crowd away.

At this moment machine gun shots were fired at the soldiers on duty at the Ministry of the Interior. The shots came from the nearby "Boteanu" apartments building located where Wilson and Boteanu streets meet. (Next day about 20 bullet marks could be seen on the ministry's walls facing Boteanu street. One bullet went as far as the building of the former Ministry for Air and the Navy, i.e. located some 200 yards north from the rear of the Ministry of the Interior where it wounded a soldier). Shots were later fired from the "Generala" and "Wilson" apartment buildings.[14]

Another wave of confusion followed. Some people dispersed and went home, others tried to hide whilst about a thousand began to force their way through the front gates of the Ministry of the Interior (facing the Royal Palace). They forced the locked gates and entered the front yard, shouting and threatening a company of soldiers under captain Teodorescu's command. The crowd ignored the placard on which was written: "Stop! Who goes beyond this point will be fired upon without further warning." Lieutenant magistrate Florin Olteanu tried to talk to any of the NDF delegates or to reach communist minister Lucrețiu Pătrășcanu. It was of no avail. Acting upon orders captain Teodorescu's company fired a volley of shots into air. Thereupon some withdrew but most seemed decided to continue.

Lieutenant Olteanu went to the intruders, talked to two of their leaders but failed to persuade them to leave the place. As the crowd had pushed its way some 30 meters into the yard, Lieutenant Olteanu assisted by major Georgescu and captain Ionescu assisted by a cordon of soldiers made another vain attempt to convince them to leave.

Consequently captain Teodorescu's company fired a second volley of warning shots. The ranks of intruders became thinner and the cordon of soldiers pushed them outside, closed and locked the gates again. "We were helped to eject the demonstrators by a Russian officer and a English officer" declared lieutenant Olteanu in his report.[15]

As things calmed down at the front gate of the Ministry of the Interior, Lieutenant Magistrate Olteanu was called outside by Mr. Constantin Agiu a communist leader and representative of the NDF. Agiu told Olteanu that there were dead and wounded. Lieutenant Olteanu asked to see them. Agiu declared that they had been already taken to the hospital. Olteanu then said that initially the NDF participants demonstrated fairly normally. But when the first shots were fired the disturbances started and people began to shout and to threaten the army "and even to fire on the soldiers".[16] Lieutenant Olteanu firmly reiterated that the soldiers had not fired at the participants, that troops had received orders to shoot into the air, "to defend themselves and to open fire only after legal warning".[17] Constantin Agiu seemed to be somehow convinced by lieutenant Olteanu's talk and went away.

Meanwhile speeches were going on the northern part of the Palace Square between the statue of King Carol I and the Athenee Palace hotel. By its very location the area was protected from snipers' fire coming from four mentioned apartment buildings.

At this time a group of some 500 persons made another attempt to force their way through the main gate of the Ministry of Internal Affairs. The soldiers fired two more volleys of warning shots into the air and intruders retreated. It has to be mentioned that during both attempts by NDF supporters to enter the ministry building by the main gate, Soviet patrols were seen preventing people from forcing their way and even dispersing them away.[18]

Whilst investigating the bullet marks in the wall of the ministry caused by shots from the Boteanu building, lieutenant magistrate Florin Olteanu witnessed NDF demonstrators running after and firing four shots at a car with high ranking officer.

The snipers' fire coming from the Ilfov, Boteanu, Generala and Wilson apartment buildings were eyewitnessed by: prosecuting magistrate Florin Olteanu, major Georgescu commander of the Interior Ministry Guard, by the commanders of the second and fourth companies of the special battalions, officers, N.C.Os, and men of the infantry gendarme regiment, also by two unidentified US officers.[19]

Toward 6:30–7:00 p.m. the demonstrators withdrew in groups shouting against the Prime minister.

There was a bloody fellow up. At 8:30 p.m. some 500 persons gathered in front of the Ministry for the Interior and expressed their support for order, for the Prime Minister and for the King. As improvised speeches went on shots were fired from the same Ilfov apartment building. Almost simultaneously a car with headlights off came from the Palace Square and moved toward Academiei street. It slowed down, put the headlights on and fired a volley of machine gun shots in demonstrators. One of them was snatched into the car. The license plate of the car has been identified as B–17094.[20]

The communist press presented the same events in a very different way. According to it, several gangs of 40–50 hooligans took the central streets Saturday evening "shouting antisemitic slogans and burning copies of the daily *Scânteia*. Not a single police officer stopped Rădescu's dear boys."[21]

Several conclusions can be drawn from the February 24 events:

1. At the beginning the NDF demonstration proceeded peacefully in the Palace Square.

2. Shots were fired on the demonstrators by unidentified snipers from the four above mentioned apartment buildings. There were eighteen casualties.

3. The NDF participants reacted believing that the army had fired. The reaction took the form of shouts, insults and pistol shots fired at the Ministry and the Royal Palace.

4. The army used their arms only when the demonstrators entered the yard of the Ministry for the Interior. The shots were fired into the air only to frighten the crowd. A representative of the Military Court and a high ranking officer were present when the warning shots were ordered

5. As soon as the snipers opened the fire, the NDF organizers threw the blame on the Prime Minister. General Rădescu was accused to have ordered the repression although events were still unfolding and no inquiry had started. It was the easiest way to confuse everyone and to "convince" the rank and file participants to the demonstration of the premier's responsibility.

6. After the communist Groza government took over there was no further inquiry on the February 24, 1945, events. The blame continued to be thrown on General Rădescu and "the fascists" backed by Maniu.

7. The causalities: two dead and sixteen wounded in the afternoon; two dead and eleven wounded in the evening. Compared to the number of the demonstrators, it seems that the afternoon shots were less aimed at

increasing the number of causalities proper but triggering and inciting the hostility of the crowd against the prime minister, Iuliu Maniu and all "fascists" and "reactionaries". The evening shots were a deliberate attempt to inflict as many causalities as possible among a small number of demonstrators. The causalities were: 18 out of some 50,000 demonstrators in the afternoon, and 13 out of about 500 in the evening.

The victims were identified, most of them were in their twenties and thirties, four of them 17–19 years old. Among them there were six workers, two ploughmen, a tailor, an accountant, a clerk, a lieutenant, a housewife, the owner of a shoe shop, and four with no specified profession. The causalities in the evening included two high school students, a policeman, a stonehewer, two drivers, a movie operator, two military men, a commercial clerk, an engineer and a man with no professional identification.[22]

The fateful Saturday knew other developments, too. At 5:40 p.m. while the shoutings were going on in the Palace Square, the Soviet military command in Bucharest sent the following order to General Rădescu, the Minister of the Interior: "General Moskvitin knows that fire arms were used in the region of the Interior Ministry, Police Headquarters, strada Clemenceau and Calea Victoria. Machine guns and hand grenades were used. The Russian command and the Allied Control Commission look upon this incident as inconsiderate and demand that fire should cease at once. If Romanian Military Command and Police Headquarters do not take immediate steps, you will bear the whole responsibility. If the firing does not cease at once, we will be compelled to intervene with our armed forces. We expect an answer by 18:00 hours."[23] In fact toward 6:30 p.m. the NDF demonstration on the Palace Square started to disband, so general Moskvitin's troops did not intervene.

A last event took place at 10 p.m. when General Rădescu broadcast to the nation. The frame up the prime minister had witnessed during the day was so cynical that he lost his temper. It was actually the last non-censored broadcast by a high ranking Romanian official for almost 45 years. He told the nation the plain and cold truth in uncompromising but extremely emotional terms. "Brother Romanians, he said, the nationless and godless as the people have described them[24], have begun to set fire to the country and to bathe it in blood. A handful of individuals, led by two foreigner Ana Pauker and Luca the Hungarian are trying to subdue the nation through terror. They shall fall crushed... Under the mask of democracy, a democracy which at each step they trample underfoot these frightful hyenas hope to obtain control of the country. Their accursed deeds are countless throughout the country..."

Then general Rădescu briefly described the events of the day. The prefecture of Craiova had been stormed by armed groups. A similar attack in

Caracal had been repelled by the military. In Bucharest shots were fired at the Royal Palace and the Ministry of the Interior. Two bullets entered the office of the marshal of the palace and another bullet fell near the prime minister's desk. Aggressors from an unidentified car fired a volley of automatic pistol on demonstrators leaving two dead and eleven wounded, at 9:30 p.m.

"The criminals who perpetrated these crimes" said the general Rădescu, "are now throwing the blame on the army which is supposed to have been the provoker".

"I affirm most emphatically that there cannot be a more infamous insinuation" continued the broadcast. "The army had my express orders not to attack unless it was attacked. Moreover, whenever troops were attacked they shot into the air only in order to intimidate the attackers."

"The black souls of the Nationless and Godless" ended Rădescu, "will burden their consciences with further crimes. These are the facts, these are the men. But can we content ourselves with pointing this out without incurring the punishment of God?"[25]

The Allied (Soviet) Control Commission (ACC) reacted promptly. Towards 11 p.m. a Soviet colonel and a lieutenant came to the interior ministry and requested general Rădescu to go to ACC on "a question of urgent and pressing importance". The prime minister accompanied by his aide-de-camp and by lieutenant colonel magistrate Oreste Dobrotescu went there and returned to the ministry after 1:00 a.m.[26]

General Rădescu was asked by the general Vinogradov, Vice-Chairman of the ACC, to explain why he had addressed the nation without prior consent of the Allied Control Commission. The following day a "rigid Soviet censorship" of all radio communications was imposed. At the same time Soviet censors in Bucharest refused to pass any press release different from the local communist version of the events.[27]

The facts stated in the emotional broadcast of the prime minister were correct. One point was however missing. Romanian communists stood firmly behind Ana Pauker and Vasile (Laszlo) Luca. Gheorghe Gheorghiu Dej, Constantin Doncea, Gh. Vasilichi, Petre Constantinescu–Iaşi, Gh. Vlădescu Răcoasa, Miron Constantinescu, not to speak of the younger Nicolae Ceauşescu, were as eager as the "foreigners" to forcibly implant the communism regime. The imposition of the communist dominated Groza government was planned and implemented by a communist minority irrespective of its ethnic background with the direct participation of the Soviet government and army.

In a written statement the National Liberal Party stressed that "will not tolerate the setting up of a new dictatorship under the cover of democracy devoid of its essential principles: liberty and order". The NLP resolutely protested against the acts of violence committed against the legal representatives of the state authority, against "the terror exercised by an aggressive minority over the working masses" in the new labor unions. The NLP also protested against the "anonymous, clandestine and illegal censorship on the part of syndicates not elected by working printers", against the "absurd and unfounded accusations" and "organized aggressions" aiming at all those who have different opinions. Thus the NLP condemned all the methods characteristic of a fascist dictatorship and warned "the people of the danger they represent for the very existence and future of the country".

The National Liberal Party approved all governmental measures for the assurance of law and order and expressed its entire support "to the union of democratic parties (NPP and, probably the Social Democrats) the only ones capable in accordance with the Yalta decisions to guarantee a democratic regime founded on order, law and liberty".[28]

The basic developments of Saturday February 24, 1945, were fully confirmed by written reports sent by the US political and by the US military representatives in Romania. The details are included in the daily telegrams.

"From the information available to this mission (US mission in Bucharest – D.C.G.) it appears clearly that the army did not fire the first shots and that when the troops did fire, they fired first into the air" concluded the US representative in Bucharest. "Doctors who treated the wounded during the evening stated emphatically to reliable informants that they (the wounds – D.C.G.) were made from pistols and other caliber weapons not used in the Romanian army."[29]

VIII. IN THE WAKE OF THE FEBRUARY 24 EVENTS

The reactions of the pro-communist press turned vitriolic and hysterical. The National Democratic Front version on the sequence and the meaning of the February 24 events was adamantly reinforced by incredibly extended comments. A *România Liberă* editorial by N. Moraru entitled: *The executioners of the people should be punished* referred to the prime minister, Iuliu Maniu and their followers as: murderer, executioner, reactionary clique, hooligan, gangs of hooligans, fascist residues, nazis, prohitlerist thugs, bandits, treacherous reactionaries, the hitlerist beasts, their hideous faces of vulgar fascists, premeditated attack, provocation, shameless provocation, assassinations, crimes, outrageous lies, base action, rascal, mean repulsive...[1] This was an absolute premiere of vulgarity, violence and obscenity in Romania's journalism. Almost no new facts were included in the communist version backed by endless comments.[2] It stubbornly alleged that the shots came from the Interior Ministry and that no provocation came from any demonstrator. This was an essential point as to throw all the blame on the government and the traditional parties, the National Peasants and the Liberals. The daily *Scânteia* read: Yesterday "executioner Rădescu organized the bloody massacre in the place square".[3] The demonstration was directed against "fascists" such as Rădescu and Maniu who "have taken a position against the decisions of the Yalta conference". The Prime Minister and his clique should be moved and "send before the People's Tribunal to account for the massacre of the nation, to account for the crimes".[4]

România Liberă printed on the front-page: "to the peaceful demonstration of over 600,000 antifascists citizens (actually no more than 50,000 – D.C.G.), Rădescu the murderer answered with volleys of machine gun fire".[5] An unidentified NDF governmental added in an interview with *Libertatea* (the social democrat daily): "There was no provocation of aggression at all from the demonstrators. Only vile liars can assert the contrary." The same leader added: "I witnessed the events and I say there is no doubt that everything took place according to a prearranged plan. General Rădescu wanted to show his strength, to intimidate us, and ordered to open fire on our peaceful demonstration."[6]

The Marshal of the Court Dumitru Negel issued a communiqué stating that: "There was no army unit in the Royal Palace during the demonstration; there was not the slightest evidence that shots had been fired from the palace; on the contrary two bullets fired upon by demonstrators hit his very office. The communiqué was censored before publication on the form that "not a single shot has been fired from the Royal Palace".[7] *Scânteia* nevertheless reacted and insisted without any proof that the shots came from the government buildings and "above all from the Royal Palace".[8] The Prime Minister's broadcast was labeled as "a speech prevaricated to the deepest impudence by the beast Rădescu".[9] This fact "finally unmasks him as a most dangerous fascist agent and an enemy of the people".[10]

The National Democratic Front issued a communiqué reiterating its sequence of events, and added that: "The government headed by Rădescu the assassin must be dismissed immediately, without an hour's delay."[11]

The nine NDF ministers of the cabinet allegedly sent a telegram to the King. They condemned the murder of "peaceful citizens", stressed that "murderers" such as Rădescu, Maniu, Negulescu, i.e. Gen. Negulescu the Minister of War and "their clique 'discredit the crown' " and demanded the immediate dismissal of Rădescu's government, the arrest and punishment of these responsible for the shootings.[12] Several days later the King was reliably reported not to have received the telegram which was printed for obvious political propaganda.[13]

In a second communiqué issued the 27th the NDF Council stated that it will continue "the resolute and all-out fight" for the formation of a NDF government. It stressed "the most perfect unity and cohesion between the parties and organizations of the NDF, despite all insinuations". United with the entire people the NDF "will mercilessly annihilate the fascists beasts!"[14] Why was this new communiqué needed? According to "reliable information" part of the Social Democrats disagreed with the Communist policies and were ready to take a stand.

It was said that the National Peasants together with the Social Democrats and the Liberals might form a coalition government without other NDF participants. The Bucharest daily *Fapta* expressed this view.[15]

In retrospect, such a move seems wishful thinking. At that time, however, the rumor was not groundless. Prior to and immediately after the February 24 demonstration the Social Democrats openly expressed their views and discontent with the Communists. Acting on behalf of the Central Committee the president of the Social Democrat Party Constantin Titel Petrescu sent a letter to the Central Committee of the Communist Party. "Friction and difficulties continue in our local and main organizations because of the sectarian and even openly hostile attitude of a numerous communist comrades toward our party"[16], wrote the social democrat leader. This attitude is illustrated by the tendency to dismiss social democrats from factories, workshops, unions and other public posts, to arrest them (cases in Oltenița, Ploiești and in the Dîmbovița county), to threaten them with "deportation to Siberia" or jail (at Bucharest tramway company, at the Moreni oil fields, at coal mines in Valea Jiului). Such actions should be rapidly brought to a halt since otherwise the United Workers' Front (agreed upon the Social Democrats and Communists on September 1, 1944) "cannot fulfill its mission".

Therefore, continued the letter, the Central Committee of the Social Democratic Party made some special proposals:

The Communist Party should take the necessary measures to ensure that its members respect the common resolution of October 2, 1944.[17] The nominations for the United Workers' Front's Committees should thus be agreed upon jointly in all centers "and particularly in Bucharest". Unilateral decisions when "one party (i.e. the Social Democrats – D.C.G.) is faced with faits accomplish by other (i.e. Communists – D.C.G.) must cease". This was especially needed in Bucharest where "certain comrades of the Communist Party systematically sabotage the United Workers' Front with intolerance and sectarism".

To put an end to all complains, friction and misunderstandings local factory and union committees should be reelected. Elections should take place on common lists but with proper representation of both parties. If there is no agreement, then the elections should proceed with secret ballot on separate lists. The new committee would be formed proportionally to the votes won by each party. The Communist Party organizations should no longer interfere with trade union matters.

The sale of *Libertatea* the Social Democrat daily paper, "is prevented by force by Communist comrades" in some factories. Such practices should also cease.

The National Democratic Front "serves party (i.e. Communist Party – D.C.G.) interests" added Constantin Titel Petrescu. The NDF should be "a form of inter-party collaboration" and not "a superimposed party". The social democrats and the communists had to maintain their individuality since the NDF program is a response to immediate needs of the country.

Moreover recent developments request a solution. "Owing to the sectarism and intolerance of provincial communist organizations, Communist prefects and mayors have been imposed" through "popular actions". This imposition went on without a "just distribution of the administrative posts between the two parties".

Furthermore, the Social Democrats oppose the unchecked censorship by printers. The censorship should be carried out by the central organ of the United Workers' Front, only. As for agrarian reform a bill must be drawn up immediately.

The letter ended by proposing a joint meeting to formulate the above mentioned principles and directives and to put them into practice.

What was Titel Petrescu hoping for when he sent the letter on behalf of the social democrat central committee? If implemented the proposals would have obviously resulted in a social democrat lead in all unions.

The Communists wouldn't have accepted a Social Democrat lead and were more than ever determined not to yield an inch. They knew that the Soviet government and army were firmly on their side.

Titel Petrescu's letter was a preliminary step. Was he ready to go further? In 1945 he did not go beyond written or privately spoken dissenting words. One year later he and his followers would end by being expelled from the party (March 1946). The letter was supposed to express some consensus of the Social Democrat Central Committee. That was no so since in 1945 the pro-communist faction was strong enough to counter any attempt to disentangle the party from communist dominance.

The letter came too late and the proposals never took shape. As February was coming to an end the Social Democrats were caught into the Communist-NDF web.

The only known reaction of the Communists to the letter was a NDF communiqué published in February 27. It stated "the most perfect unity and cohesion" of the NDF parties and organizations despite all insinuations. As usual the communist media general wording concealed complex contradictory realities.

The NDF propaganda barrage continued increasingly. Six generals, three colonels and a major protested against the Prime Minister's broadcast on February 24: "We break off with General Rădescu's deeds and statements which are harmful to the army's and country's interests. We are and remain loyal to His Majesty King Mihai I and to the Romanian people to whom we have sworn faithfulness." Thus ten out of thousands of Romanian high ranking officers sided with the Communist lead NDF. They were immediately dropped from the army list by a decision of the Romanian Army Superior Council. Their reintegration will soon follow with the imposition of the Dr. Petre Groza government. Eight out of 114 members of the Romanian Academy expressed their anti-Rădescu protest in a telegram sent to the King.[18]

Scânteia published a letter in which General Rădescu's son allegedly threw the blame for the recent events in his father.[19]

Two key words ostensibly came out in all communists statements and comments: *premeditated provocation* as the beginning of a *civil war*. Accountable were the prime minister, the leaders of the National Peasants and Liberal Parties, especially Iuliu Maniu, and "all reactionaries" and "fascists".

The two key words had previously been expressed by NDF council's statement following the incidents at the Malaxa factory. Yet at that moment the facts could not match such assertions although the communist leaders were prone to any distortions and lies.

Now, with two people dead and sixteen wounded at the February 24, NDF demonstration the stage was set.

Civil war and/or *premeditated provocation* were reiterated in two statements of the NDF Council, the NDF telegram sent to the King, and the comments of the controlled press, starting February 25: "Rădescu has attempted to trigger the civil war"[20]... "A military pronunciamento".[21]

During the February 24 events at the Palace Square Lucrețiu Pătrășcanu, the Communist Justice Minister, told the crowd: "...They (i.e. governmental forces – D.C.G.) have shamelessly fired at the people. The government is headed by a criminal who has to be ousted. Those who ordered this, who carried out the orders, those who are actually responsible will pay with their heads. We have been provoked. We have been met by firearm shots while demonstrating peacefully. From this very moment everyone has to be a fighter for the achievement of genuine democracy (i.e. the communist rule – D.C.G.). General Rădescu cannot stay as head of the government any longer. He must go. A National Democratic Front, a genuine people's government must come for it alone will be able of weeding out the fascists."[22] "There has been a coward provocation against the people" added Pătrașcu (a representative of NDF).[23] "Rădescu must go... Do not retaliate to the provocation of those assassins... The murderer Rădescu has fired machine guns shots at the workers to save his head..." added the communist leader Constantin Doncea.[24] Gheorghiu Dej took up: "Comrades, citizens, we have been provoked. We wanted to demonstrate peacefully and shots were fired upon us. You did not provoke at all."[25]

The Communist leaders made such assertions whilst the events were developing in much confusion at the Royal Palace Square, with no official inquiry and no evidence.

The stress on *premeditated provocation* and *civil war* was not accidental. They were connected to "the purging of fascists still very active" and to the "complete and sincere fulfillment of the armistice terms" sabotaged by "reactionaries". These were four key ideas for the scenario of the communist take over. The more such public statements, the more likely was an overt Soviet intervention for the Communist lead National Democratic Front.

Within the Communist Party some were however aware of what lied behind the scenario. Iosif Szraer, general secretary at the Interior Ministry, privately talked to prince Barbu Știrbey after the February 24 shootings (sometimes on February 25–27). The two had first met in late 1943 or early 1944, prior to Știrbey's departure for the armistice talks in Cairo.[26]

Szraer frankly told Ştirbey: 1. The communists are well aware that the armistice terms had been more than fulfilled since September 1944. They assert the contrary, as a potent political weapon against the Rădescu coalition government. 2. Szraer admitted that General Rădescu was "an able an honest patriot". There was a deliberate communist scheme to compromise him. This is why the controlled press and radio repeatedly shouted "murderer" at the prime minister. 3. The communist leadership knew that the army did not shot at the demonstrators on February 24. However an all-out propaganda was launched to make the country believe that the army had. 4. The communists were better armed than people generally suspected.[27]

The Soviet media overtly backed the communist onslaught on the Romanian government with the same distorted and inverted sequence of events.

On February 27, 1945, the day of Vishinsky's arrival in Bucharest, radio Moscow broadcast: "According to the Bucharest newspapers, on February 24, National Democratic Front meetings took place in other towns also, in Craiova, Caracal, Braşov and other places. Everywhere the participants demanded the ousting of Rădescu's government." "In Bucharest fire arm and machine gun shots have been fired at the demonstrators from the Royal Palace, the Ministry of the Interior and the Police Headquarters. There are dead and wounded among the workers."

"The perpetrator of these crimes is General Rădescu and his clique, headed by Maniu. By their criminal deeds they try to nullify the August 23 act when a new life for Romania among the united nations opened."

"The NDF ministers sent a written protest requesting the King to stand against the nefarious deeds of Rădescu and Maniu and their fascists clique."

"The Rădescu government must go since it is unable to meet people's demands."

"We appeal to a peaceful population to do its utmost to force Rădescu out and to set a democratic government which would bring Romanian within the United Nations.[28]

Graiul Nou the Romanian language paper of the Red Army completely upheld the local communist version of the shooting and declared it vital to purge the fascists and to replace the Rădescu government by one able to carry out the needed reforms. The developments, added the newspaper, had become a matter of grave concern to the Soviet government.[30]

Another editorial of the same paper added: "Some responsible factors in Romania wholly disregarded the realities of Romanian policy by granting open support to the Romanian fascists." It was the country's duty to get rid of the fascists and legionaries. *Graiul Nou* urged the purge of the Romanian army of its conservative officers so that no sabotage and opposition acts could be carried out in the rear of the front line.

On March 1 and 2 the Moscow press published five TASS reports and one Red Star comment on the Romanian events. All expressed a sharp condemnation of the Rădescu's policies and stressed the need for the NDF government.[31]

During the fateful February 1945 events, the mood of the Romanian public opinion moved from hope to apprehension, uneasiness and fear.

The overwhelming majority truly believed in a coalition government with all parties represented and took the Yalta declaration at face value. As the communist thrust increased every day the public mood turned to pessimism and even apathy.[193]

There was a growing feeling that the censorship had became harsher than during the Antonescu regime. There was a growing awareness that the traditional values, way of life and realities were at stake.

IX. THE ALLIED (SOVIET) CONTROL COMMISSION ON THE ROMANIAN SITUATION

When, where and by whom was the pattern of the February events designed? The essential target of the communist lead NDF was the dismissal of the coalition government and its replacement by a National Democratic Front cabinet. The developments and facts had to be presented in such a manner as to throw discredit and blame on the Prime Minister and the traditional political parties. The above mentioned developments took place against the background of a lost war with all its consequences, the almost total control of the Romanian administration by the occupant, a strict Soviet censorship of the media, and Moscow's ultimate intent to impose a new system in the "liberated" countries. What, then, was the reality of the Allied Control Commission (ACC), supposed to represent the three big war allies and to direct Romanian affairs during the armistice phase? Nominally the ACC was a tripartite body but in fact a Soviet tool with Western representatives as observers.

The talks within the ACC couldn't solve anything. The discussions showed that: 1. The Western representatives were aware of the real meaning of the events; 2. The Soviets limited themselves to makeshift answers, and 3. The Soviet authorities backed and probably master-minded the communist lead National Democratic Front policies.

On February 14, 1945, an ACC meeting took place in Bucharest. C.V.R. Schuyler, US army chief military representative, Pavlov, Soviet political advisor and Soviet Admiral Bogdenko were present.

Approximately one hour was devoted to a "detailed discussion" of the current Romanian political situation. Some excerpts are significant:

General Schuyler: "Though there are many variations of opinion among different groups, the basic question can be solved into a fundamental difference between two separate point of view: on one hand the National Democratic Front parties desire to replace the present government by one of their own in which no other parties are represented; on the other hand, the present government desires that the nation be administrated by a coalition government in which all parties are represented."

Pavlov: "The same question has been talked over recently in detail with general Rădescu and Mr. Vișoianu (the Minister of Foreign Affairs of the Rădescu government – D.C.G.). These gentlemen were informed that the Allied Control Commission can have nothing whatsoever to do with the conduct of the internal political affairs of the various parties in Romania or with the attitude or actions of the King in his dealings with their parties. Under no circumstances will the ACC participate in such internal affairs."

"However, *no disorder can be permitted to occur in the rear of the Soviet armies... nor can any fascist activities within the state of Romania be permitted.*" (my italics D.C.G.)

Pavlov added: "*I do not feel there is a serious crisis between the NDF parties and the present government*, and such a crisis should not occur *unless General Rădescu himself brings it on.*" (my italics D.C.G.) The Soviet Counselor then embarked on a rhetorical approach to the internal Romanian problems. "What actually do the Romanian people desire?" asked Pavlov who immediately offered the answer: "...the present government in many respects does not understand the true desire of the people... as a proof there is Rădescu's attitude towards the land reform". Besides "within the present government there are still many fascists and fascists sympathizers holding important positions... The Romanian people expect the government to rid itself of these fascist elements."

Therefore "the Armistice Control Commission thinks that if such questions cannot be decided by the government, *they will be decided by the people themselves*".[1] (my italics D.C.G.).

Brigadier general C.V.R. Schuyler referred to the declaration issued by allied leaders at the Crimea Conference with full adherence to the principles of the Atlantic Charter. Therefore the ACC responsibility is to insure the existence of a coalition government with all parties represented. In view of the present political unrest "...a public announcement of the attitude of the ACC in this matter would have a definitely stabilizing effect".

Pavlov's answer was that "...any such announcement at this time would be a great mistake since, by its very declaration, the Allied Control Commission would appear to recognize that a condition of instability exists... *in the present situation no such critical situation does exist*, therefore no such statement is called for".[2] (my italics D.C.G.).

General brigadier Schuyler made the a last attempt and asked what would be the attitude of the ACC (Soviet) "in the event that any political party or group of parties in Romania should attempt to take control of the government by force?"

Counselor Pavlov: "Such a question is I believe purely academic and I do not believe we should attempt to answer it here. I do not think there is danger of any such coup d'état."[3]

The sum up, the Soviet reading of the Romanian situation on February 14, 1945, included the following:

1. There is no political crisis although the communist lead NDF had aggressively acted to get the dismissal of the Rădescu coalition cabinet.

2. The Rădescu government is unable to understand and to carry out the "urgent requirements" of the masses.

3. The Romanian administration has to be purged of fascist elements.

4. There is no political crisis "unless general Rădescu brings it on".

5. The ACC will not permit disorders or fascist activities in the rear of the front lines.

6. Otherwise the Allied (Soviet) Control Commission has nothing to do with Romanian internal politics.

Such statements represent a summit of hypocrisy. The ACC discussion on February 14, 1945, events also reveals that the Romanian communists' scenario was fully approved by probably masterminded the Soviet authorities.

The next day general Schuyler cabled a summary of the talks ending with the following comment: "I left the discussion with the clear impression that the Russians regard the left wing parties alone as voicing the true desires of the great majority of the Romanian people, and that they considered the historic parties and the army as having fascists tendencies which are highly detrimental to the war effort and dangerous to all the allied nations in general, and to Soviet Russia in particular." The Soviet perspective on and interpretation of the events was also expressed by general Vinogradov to members of the Romanian government.[4]

There was another meeting on February 20, 1945, at noon attended by Soviet Lieutenant General Vinogradov, Deputy Chairman of ACC Vice Admiral Bogdenko, Air Vice Marshal Stevenson – the British commissioner, Brigadier General Schuyler – chief US representative.[5]

Several issues were focused on, among which the freedom of the press. Air Vice Marshal Stevenson referred to the suppression of the newspapers by ACC: "...the actual effect is the restriction of the expression of certain important political parties in the country whilst... none of NDF papers have ever been suppressed." The Soviet censorship "has rather expanded and seems to be little one-sided" added the British air vice marshal. Since "...there is a virtual suppression of the party organs[6] with the exception of the National Democratic Front". Therefore permits to publish papers should be granted in all places where they are requested "...so that different political parties are able to express their opinions".[7]

General Vinogradov: "Any paper will be suppressed which might start raising fascist propaganda in this country... in several cases articles have been printed which we considered to be so disgusting that the papers had to be closed." The Soviet deputy chairman of the ACC gave no examples.[8]

The three senior representatives of the ACC discussed at length a letter from Moldavia printed by *Dreptatea* and considered by the Soviet censors to include a coded message.[9] Regarding the incidents at the Malaxa factory which took place the very day of the ACC meeting, general Vinogradov said that the ACC should not interfere with the matter. His statement was duly approved by the US and UK representatives.[10]

Two Russian officers were however sent to the Malaxa plant to assess the situation and implicitly to sent a sign to the Romanian authorities.[11] Moreover, general Rădescu was summoned to the ACC on February 19, and told that the Soviets "*would not permit under any circumstances a civil war in Romania*, as this would damage the general aspects of the war against Hitler".[12] (my italics D.C.G.).

General Vinogradov continued: "The position in this country is very, very tense, the danger is great. The Prime Minister has given the order that demonstrators would be fired at. If that is the case, *it must mean the beginning of civil war.* (my italics D.C.G.) I asked Rădescu yesterday quite clearly whether he wants civil war. He answered that he does not. *Certain events may lead to civil war. The Prime Minister says that he does not want it but if circumstances led to it, then there is nothing that can be done about it. Under these circumstances he (Rădescu) could not govern the country*". (my italics D.C.G.). In general Vinogradov's opinion of the "agrarian question", the land reform, was the main problem from which "all of the other misunderstandings are arising".[13] He added that "not a single person in the National Democratic Front wants the civil war".[14] Towards the end of the meeting, he warned again: "If the Prime Minister (Rădescu) permits the outbreak of the civil war in the country, I doubt very much whether he is a satisfactory minister. I don't know. You gentlemen should think that over." The Soviet representative sided with the NDF version of events and strongly raised the perspective of the civil war in Romania.

The ACC meeting also discussed a third issue. In some localities "certain groups of people" had attempted "to take over unlawfully the functions of the national government". The topic was raised by General Brigadier Schuyler who submitted a draft declaration of the ACC aimed at effectively contributing to the political stability of the country. The declaration stated that:

1. Following the terms of the Yalta agreement, the ACC has the responsibility to insure the existence of a coalition government in which all the political parties are represented.

2. Under these conditions, the Romanian state under its King is entirely free to select its governmental representatives. Such a government should be able to maintain internal order and to fulfill armistice terms.

3. Any attempt by individuals or political parties to overthrow the government or any of its agencies by force will be considered by ACC as an act of sabotage against the war effort. Such attempts will therefore not be tolerated. Political or other demonstrations during working hours are not favourable looked upon by the ACC. The mass meetings and "political maneuverings" should not "be permitted to interfere with the war effort".[15]

Air Vice Marshal Stevenson on behalf of His Majesty's Government supported "in full and in every detail what General Schuyler has said".[16] If adopted such a declaration would have brought to a halt or considerably delayed the communists' assault on the legal authorities. Accordingly it would have reinforced a coalition cabinet as the one headed by General Rădescu.

General Vinogradov's answer was non committal. "I talked about such a declaration with General Rădescu. I will examine this suggestion and will of course give you an answer... Perhaps the existing government does not satisfy the people..." True this cabinet include all parties but" added General Vinogradov "it will take 25 years before it functions".[17] In Soviet views General Rădescu was almost out: "there must be a strong man there who comes to this sort of business, the way you gentlemen here have agreed to prevent a civil war. That is the kind of man who should be at the head of it".

The ACC meeting ended inconclusively. The Soviet inflexibility made it impossible to move forward on vital issues such as liberty of the opposition press and the continuation of a coalition government.

Prior to any investigation, General Vinogradov considered the Premier Rădescu as inciting to an impending civil war, and being unable to prevent it.

The Soviet views were almost identical to those expressed by the Romanian Communists and their controlled press.

There was a follow up next day, February 21, 1945. The ACC met briefly for 45 minutes, at 8:40 p.m., seemingly at the request of General Brigadier C.V.R. Schuyler.[18] He reiterated his request to make public an ACC statement as proposed the day before which would "insure the preservation of a reasonable amount of stability in government". General Schuyler told his colleagues about *Scânteia* editorial printed that very day (February 21, 1945) which is "an incentive to the people to rise up and actually cause a revolution". The *Scânteia* editorial was giving the communist version of the Malaxa plant incidents: "While they shot at us, the fascists shouted... The criminals opened fire... Not only did the bandits not fear the intervention of the police or of the army, they obviously relied on their help. Although the whole city knew and was talking about what was happened at Malaxa's no troops appeared before 11 o'clock, to prevent the fascists from shooting at us... The United Workers' Front calls on all the workers to repeal with the utmost determination the provocation and attacks of the fascists bands. Let us answer with ten blows to one blow of the fascists!" The title of the editorial was inflammatory: "A group of fascists armed with crowbars, hand grenades and automatic pistols, inspired by Maniu and instigated by Rădescu, tried to seize the Malaxa plant yesterday. Comrade Gheorghe Apostol... was seriously wounded. The heroic intervention of the workers of Bucharest."[19] "Do you not think" added general Schuyler "that something ought to be done to prevent further publication of provocative articles of this nature at this time?" General Vinogradov said that he has not read the article and that he cannot take a decision by himself. General Schuyler's proposal on a joint ACC statement was forwarded to Moscow... "And I am now awaiting the answer, Moscow is aware of the political situation here."[20]

The Soviet representative referred to the Crimean Declaration which dealt with the liberated and satellite countries. He read the corresponding paragraph[21] and added: "it is exceptionally well written". "From this I consider that the general policy in such cases has been fixed by the Crimean Conference. It is a broad policy."

With regard to recent Romanian developments, general Vinogradov said: "The responsibility for order in the country belongs to Rădescu as the head of the government... The Allied Control Commission is not going to give him any hints on how to go about it. It is up to him to decide how to do it. If it were the policy of the ACC to settle all internal problems of the government, we might do away with the government and let the Allied Control Commission run the country... It is an internal problem and the ACC does not intend to meddle with internal policy.[22]

Thus on one hand, the Romanian Communists and their satellites in full agreement with the Soviet authorities, were inciting every day to more demonstrations and public unrest aiming at leading to the control of local authorities. On the other hand, according to Soviet views, the responsibility for law and order rested entirely with Premier Rădescu who in turn was inciting to civil war, or conversely unable to prevent it.

The British representative replied that the developments in Romania were precisely typical of the situations as specified by the declaration of Crimea: "I believe" added air vice marshal Stevenson "that general Schuyler's paper raised a very important principle and the principle was that in case of any other incident, it was for the ACC to administer the policy that I just referred to".

General Vinogradov was not impressed: "The whole country (i.e. Romania), the nation itself is at stake, and the problem must be referred to the Moscow government. The decision cannot be made here... When the proper time comes, the proper actions will be taken."

"In the meantime, the measures which have been taken (by ACC) are sufficient. The government has been notified, and there is nothing to do but wait for decision of the Moscow Government."

The decision did not take a long time to come. It was expressed one week later by a special Soviet envoy, the deputy minister for foreign affairs, Andrey Yanuarevich Vishinsky.

However the British ACC representative made another attempt. He endorsed general Schuyler's suggestion to take action against the daily *Scânteia* for its incendiary editorial. There is a good case against the paper and "it would have a good deal of effect and would do no harm to anyone in the country" added the British senior high ranking officer.

General Vinogradov: "For three or four days?"

Air vice marshal Stevenson: "Well, even for a day, the effect would be good."

General Vinogradov did not move an inch. He promised to look into *Scânteia* editorial. The main reason for closing down a newspaper is "fascist and nazi propaganda". The Soviet general did not explain what fascist or nazi propaganda meant.

"Any individual who writes an inflammatory article aimed at inciting to open rebellion at the critical time, is actually one of those individuals ready to hinder allies' war effort" – replied the US representative.[23]

With this ACC meeting was over.

With the Soviet undisputed command within ACC and the Soviet troops in full control of Romania, the local communists went ahead with their plans as shown by the events of February 24, 1945.

Nevertheless the UK representative made another attempt. He sent the Soviets a note on the incidents at the Malaxa factory (on February 19–20, 1945). What happened there wasn't "...anything more than a small scale riot which as such was within the authority of the civil power to quell. The civil power (i.e. Rădescu government) accordingly dealt with the situation and restored order". "Such facts" added the British note "are endemic to industrialized countries in Europe." Once satisfactorily dealt with it is "in the view of His Majesty's government" that such incidents could not "*be regarded as a state of civil war and therefore a menace to the security of the lines of communications with the Russian armies which run through Romania.*"[24] (my italics D.C.G.). General brigadier C.V.R. Schuyler also made an attempt to inform the Soviet colleague of the official US position with regard to events in Romania, namely:

1. The best way to have representative administration in Romania is a coalition government including all political groups and social classes. Until free elections are held, the US administration does not wish to see an exclusively National Peasant or a National Democrat Front government and would particularly deplore to use and display of force to bring any party into power.

2. Any attempt to bring local or central administrative changes through force and other disorderly means cannot be tolerated.

3. No political party or organization should be allowed to have armed units. "All instruments of force should be at the government's disposal only. The legal authorities should have adequate means to maintain internal order at their disposal."[25]

A week earlier, on February 20, 1945, Brigadier General C.V.R. Schuyler sent the War Department a long telegram expressing his views on the situation on Romania based on a careful evaluation of all available information: "...Soviet Russia has been following a definite and carefully conceived program designed sooner or later to lead to the disintegration of the historic political parties (NPP and NLP) in Romania, and to the creation of a situation on which only the extreme leftist government will be capable of maintaining order and directing the nation's affairs."[26] The final goal is "the transformation of Romania into an independent communistic state friendly to, and economically dependent on Russia".[27] At this time the stage was gradually set for the appointment of a leftist government based on "popular" demand. Several developments are pointing to the outcome:

1. Continued attacks in the local and Soviet communist press on Iuliu Maniu and other leaders of the National Peasant Party (NPP).

2. The suppression of several NPP newspapers and the introduction of a "rigid censorship" so that the public receive news from the pro-communist media only.

3. "Extremely rigid" Soviet censorship over all outgoing news cables coupled with the ACC refusal to grant US or British correspondents entry visas in Romania.

4. Gradual reduction by Soviet ACC orders of Romanian home forces to the point where such forces may be unable to suppress well planned and organized disorders.

5. Continued official relations of ranking Soviet officers and diplomats with Romanian communist leaders or affiliates, in contrast to Vishinsky's refusal to grant an audience to Maniu.

6. Continuation of various harsh Soviet policies which are leading to the disruption on the Romanian traditional economic and social fabric. The most recent examples were the ruthless deportation of Germans and Bessarabians, and the establishment of an arbitrary and abnormal ruble–leu exchange rate.[28] Additionally, the Soviet authorities did not set any dates for the Romanian administration to go back in Northern Transylvania, for the release of Romanian war prisoners (including over 100,000 taken after the August military coup), for the beginning of Romania's trade relations with other countries.

The Allied Control Commission is an agency which hands all Soviet demands and directives over to the Romanian government. The orders, continued general Schuyler, were issued without prior consent or at least knowledge of the US or UK representatives. Yet, the Romanian public opinion believe that US and UK governments have a share in the policies instrumented and implemented by ACC.

Not astoninglishly, a growing sense of gloom, incertitude and fear loomed in people's minds.[29]

The Queen mother (Elena former wife of the ex-king Carol II, and Mother of King Mihai of Romania) told General Schuyler on February 19, that the "leftist parties would soon attempt some sort of coup d'état would otherwise gain control of the government".[30] The evolution might lead to a critical situation when the very lives of the Royal family could be threatened. The Queen Mother requested the Western allies to grant the King and herself protection.

General Schuyler's reply was noncommittal. He requested however instructions since he felt that "at any time the situation may begin to deteriorate rapidly".[31] A few days later he suggested (in agreement with Burton Berry, US political representative in Bucharest) "in the event of serious local disorders", to grant asylum in buildings occupied by US agencies, to individuals "who we feel have either made a outstanding contribution to the allied cause or have risked their lives in assisting American prisoners of war".[32]

The acting Secretary of State referred in his answer to the Yalta Declaration of February 12, 1945, on liberated countries in Europe as well as to Molotov's statement of April 2, 1944, that the USSR is not following the aim of "making changes in Romania's existing social structure". If the communists in Romania do try to seize power, continued the acting Secretary of State, "this is a matter of concern to all three major allies. Should the King's personal safety be threatened, or his Mother's, the responsibility for making sure of their safety by furnishing either protection or means of getting out of Romania ought to rest on ACC". The US Government should not offer protection independently. General Schuyler had no authority to protect the Royal family to an extent beyond his functions as representative in ACC.[33]

When the letter with the US position on developments in Romania was officially transmitted to the Allied (Soviet) Control Commission in Bucharest on February 27, 1945, the dice had been already cast.

X. THE DISMANTLEMENT AND DISARMAMENT OF THE ROMANIAN HOME FORCES

It all started in the fall of 1944. On August 23, 1944 the Romanian Army had 29 fully equipped divisions: 18 infantry divisions, 1 guard, 4 mountain, 5 cavalry, 1 armored. The armistice agreement (signed on Moscow on September 12, 1944) stated Romania's military participation against the nazi Reich at a minimum of 12 divisions.[1] Therefore the Romanian delegation for the signature of the Armistice Convention raised the issue of a military convention between the two armies. Molotov's opinion was that the matter has to be settled at a later date. Meanwhile the Soviets took prisoners as many as possible although the Romanian units had stopped fighting against the Soviet on August 23 at midnight. The remaining Romanian force were integrated into the second Ukrainian Front under the high command of marshal Malinovsky. These troops had heavy casualties and more men were needed for replacements.

On September 25, 1944, the Soviet command drafted a protocol which ordered the disbandment of all major units of the Romanian home army. The Romanian delegation rejected the Soviet order and the discussions were interrupted, then resumed on October 23, 1944. The Soviets' view was to allow only three divisions as strategic reserve for the Romanian Army (and not ten divisions as requested by the Romanian General Staff).

On October 25, 1944, the Soviet Command told the Romanians that the conditions are final, and cannot be changed. If not accepted the consequences would be "serious up to the demobilization, even to the dismantlement by Soviet forces of all major Romanian units not needed on the front line".

The chief of Romanian General Staff, General Nicolae Rădescu reluctantly signed the protocol. He stated in written that the protocol "had been imposed by the Allied (Soviet) Control Commission", and added that Soviets' order is contrary to the Armistice Convention. In General Gheorghe Mihail's opinion Soviet Marshal Malinovsky wanted to prevent any Romanian armed opposition to the increased and repeated Soviet orders. Thus the demobilization of 13 divisions of the Romanian home army had to be completed on December 1, 1944.[2] The move was aimed at possibly depriving any Romanian coalition government of any forces able to react to orchestrated internal disorders.

The "disturbances" were essential for the communist takeover scenario. They were meant to "prove" the inefficiency and/or unwillingness of the coalition government to maintain order. A further reduction of the traditional police and gendarmerie was a green light for increased pre-planned disorders.

On February 14, 1945, at the Allied (Soviet) Control Commission meeting General Brigadier C.V.R. Schuyler said that the Romanian authorities had been called upon by several ACC directives, to operate further reductions of the home forces, the gendarmes and frontier guards. "Numerous Romanians" continued the US representative, told him that the army's home units are "insufficient to cope with any serious or organized disorders".[3]

But Soviet Counselor Pavlov saw it otherwise. The reductions "were determined by mutual agreement with the Romanian government and no serious protest against these reductions has been received".[4] Besides, added Counselor Pavlov and Vice Admiral Bogdenko (Naval Aide to Marshal Malinovski, Chairman of the ACC in Romania), "the apparent desire of some Romanians for a larger rear area force indicates that they contemplate using such a force against the Romanian people themselves".[5]

According to Soviet estimations, the strength of the Romanian Army amounted to 14 divisions on the battle front, i.e. 123,000 men; three divisions in the rear for front line replacements "plus supply troops, miscellaneous etc"., i.e. 380,000 men; in all 503,000 men.

"This in itself is evidence" continued Counselor Pavlov "that some high ranking officers in the Romanian Army are actually sabotaging the execution of the military protocol (i.e. signed in October 25, 1944, – D.C.G.), by maintaining huge forces in the rear, probably for nefarious purposes. Such forces could be used only against the Romanian people themselves, or against the allied nations. Since either such employment obviously would be inconceivable for a democratic state, we must conclude that this situation is the result of fascist influence... There are so many (Romanian) officers in Bucharest that they crowd the streets and get in each other's way. This situation is deplorable."[6]

Vice admiral Bogdenko echoed his colleague. The presence "of over 100 tanks" in Bucharest is another indication of the existence in the Romanian Army of "fascist sympathizers" who are "probably planning" something "against the Romanian people or against the allied themselves at a later date".

The US Military Mission in Bucharest had different data. In the first half of February 1945, the Romanian Army had 417,000 men as compared to 866,000 before August 23, 1944. 174,000 were on the front as follows: First Army – 49,000; Forth Army – 71,000; Rear Echelon – 10,000; troops in transit – 24,000; bridge river unit – 2,000; road battalions – 4,000; railway units – 6,000; wounded – 8,000.

The remaining 243,000 were within the country namely: reserve depots – 69,000; General Staff, Royal House and Military center of

Bucharest – 11,000; third army – 25,000; military schools – 55,000; gendarmes – 32,000; border guards – 26,000; Ministry of War Production – 4,000; wounded – 29,000.[7]

Irrespective of the figures the Soviet authorities wanted to emphasize the "reality" of a "fascist" threat, of "planned hostile actions" against the Romanian people, of disorders in the rear of the frontier.

Such "threats" and "disorders" would have enabled the Soviets to invoke the provisions of the armistice convention and thus to impose the dismissal of the Rădescu government.

At the following ACC meeting of February 20, 1945, Vice admiral Bogdenko reiterated the number of Romanian troops on the front and in the rear and added: "In every corner of Bucharest there are five officers. In the restaurants there are 30 officers. These figures will give you an idea how the Romanians are fighting the war."[8]

Such complains were seemingly voiced more than once. According to General Schuyler's report of March 25, 1945, "the Russian Allied Control Commission personnel maintains that the morale of these units (i.e. Romanian units – D.C.G.) is extremely low and the most officers and men have lost interest in the war".[9] US military representative added that from the information the US Mission had received, "many of these Romanian divisions (14 on the battlefront – D.C.G.) are in very bad shape. This is due to lack of transport, equipment and supplies, *large quantities of which are seized by the Russians although destined for Romanians*". (my italics D.C.G.)

There was more in the same US report: "All the Romanian officers from the front with whom we have talked complain that *the Russians show Romanian units no consideration whatsoever and merely use them as cannon fodder. They are thrown into attack after attack with inadequate support, suffer heavy casualties, and are given no opportunity for rest and refitting. The men are thus exhausted physically and morale is very low.*"[10] (my italics D.C.G.).

While the Soviet representatives blamed many of the Romanian officers, the Soviet commanders on the front repeatedly cited the Romanian troops for their courage and bravery.[11]

The final move for the reduction of the Romanian home forces took place on March 1, 1945. The Allied (Soviet) Control Commission issued 8 separate orders as follows:

1. 20,000 officers and men of the Romanian air forces and 170 planes are to be demobilized. It included two fighter groups, five transport groups, one training squadron, one liaison squadron, one balloon squadron, one guard battalion, one service units, six antiaircraft batteries with 60 guns.

2. The infantry guard regiment from Bucharest (about 2,100 men) is to be sent to the front immediately since it refused to be disarmed.

3. Reserve battalions of all regiments now at the front are to be disbanded and their personnel to be sent to the battle lines.

4. The gendarmes, i.e. forces to maintain the internal order, to be reduced from 31,000 to 14,500. All schools for gendarme officers and non-commissioned officers to be closed.

5. One regiment of the frontier guards to be demobilized. Another frontier guard regiment stationed in Bucharest to be sent in the countryside, but one company about 250 men to remain in the capital to guard banks, financial institutions etc.

6. An immediate 50 per cent reduction in the country's police forces down to 7,500 men, 1,500 of whom possibly in Bucharest (at that time Bucharest had about 1,000,000 inhabitants).

7. All fire arms to be removed at once from different Bucharest units such as: fire brigade, three battalions guarding the War Ministry, the General Staff Headquarters, and administrative buildings, an auto repair battalion, three detachments for the War Production Ministry and for Constructions, i.e. in all 9,561 men.

8. Machine guns and automatic weapons to be removed from all buildings.[12]

During the first day of March 1945, the demobilization and the disarming of Romanian troops in Bucharest went on rapidly under Soviet direction on behalf of the Allied Control Commission. All materials and weapons were collected in designed dumps to be sent to the main Soviet depot at Cotroceni. All activities were under Soviet supervision, and all collecting points under Soviet military guard.[13]

The Romanian General Staff sent a written protest to General Vinogradov, Deputy Chairman of the ACC on March 5, 1945. The pro test pointed out all the very negative consequences of the ACC order, and added: "...the Romanian Army shouldn't be forced to such contradictory standards; comrades submitted to continuous efforts on the battlefront, object of capture, of disarmament and vexation on the Romanian territory proper".[14]

The same day March 1st, the Soviet military took over most of the transmission facilities of the Romanian air staff. They included the ground stations of the First Romanian Air Corps on the front line as well as in Bucharest. In this way the Romanian Air Staff was left with one teletype circuit relay Bucharest – Brașov – Cluj – Oradea and one telegraph line for two–three night hours only. Telegrams were thus transmitted to Oradea and from there to units by automobile, or by any other available means including horseback. All flights of Romanian personnel within the country (except for military couriers) were also stopped by Soviet order.

On February 28 in the morning, i.e. the day after Vishinsky's arrival, it was generally reported that some 6,000 Soviet troops had moved into Bucharest to be soon followed by some 4,000 NKDV men. All were billeted in the capital and in its suburbs. During the night of 27 to 28 of February and the next morning Soviet armed patrols were very much in evidence. In the following day Russian patrols with automatic weapons were greatly strengthened in the city and frequently seen on the streets.[15] Marshal Rodion Malinovsky, Chairman of the ACC arrived in Bucharest joined by his Deputy Chairman General Vinogradov who had just returned from Moscow. Both were reported to be in town in February 28, 1945.[16]

The commander of the Bucharest Soviet troops issued an order requesting a special written permit for any vehicle to be driven at night.[17] On March 5, 1945, the capital city of Romania was a virtually cordoned off area, tightly controlled by the Soviet Army.

The confusion and tension increased and rumors spread about a direct Soviet intervention.[18]

The stage was thus set for the communist take over. One additional but essential move was however needed. At this very moment Andrey Januarevich Vishinsky stepped in.

XI. VISHINSKY IMPOSES A COMMUNIST LEAD GOVERNMENT

The Soviet Deputy Foreign Minister Andrey Januarevitch Vishinsky unexpectedly arrived in Bucharest in the evening of February 27, 1945. He asked to be immediately received by the King.

The direct Soviet intervention was essential for the communist take over. Otherwise it would have been impossible for the Communist Party of Romania to impose its government.

Vishinsky's audience with King Mihai took place on February 27, 1945, at 9 p.m. Romanian Foreign Minister Constantin Vişoianu and N. Negel Marshal of the Royal Court were also present.

The Rădescu Government, said A.J. Vishinsky, proved unable to keep the internal order, had no mass support, and took "reactionary measures" against the people.

Romanian is close to the front-line, continued the Soviet Deputy Commissar for Foreign Affairs, and "we (the Soviets) are highly interested to see order and peace in this area".

"Isn't your Majesty aware of the need to immediately dismiss the Rădescu Government and to replace it by a Cabinet of the democratic parties and of independent persons relying on the confidence and willingness of the broad masses?"

"I have started consultations" replied King Mihai. "Besides, one has to take into account the Yalta Declaration."

Vishinsky: "There is nothing on the Rădescu Government in the Yalta Declaration. I'd like to know your Majesty's decision on the two above mentioned problems (i.e. the dismissal of the Rădescu Cabinet and the appointment of a new one – D.C.G.) and to report it to my Government."

The Romanian Foreign Minister Constantin Vişoianu tried with no results to explain the country's constitutional procedures when a new Prime Minister and a new Cabinet are appointed.

A. Vishinsky: "In the circumstances, and expressing my Government opinion also, we have (i.e. Soviet Government – D.C.G.) the right to intervene for our common sake, for us and Romania whom we wish only good. We cannot accept reactionary and even prohitlerist demonstrations in a country next to our front lines."[1]

The second meeting took place next day February 28, 1945, at 3:30 p.m. Constantin Vişoianu Minister for Foreign Affairs, and D. Negel Marshal of the Royal Court were also present.

A.J. Vishinsky focused on two points: "We (the Soviet government – D.C.G.) consider general Rădescu as fascist and his government also fascist or at least backing fascists... On my Government's behalf I officially declare you that we cannot tolerate such a Cabinet... The situation cannot last any longer and we think it necessary to change the government immediately. Till 6 p.m. today the Cabinet's resignation should be announced. The appointment of a new premier should follow immediately."[2]

The second Vishinsky's demand was the immediate reinstallment of the ten high ranking Romanian officers who sided with the NDF in a written statement. The King had to agree.[3]

The third audience took place next day, March 1, 1945, at 10 p.m. "We want a trustworthy Government... On behalf of my Government I have to tell Your Majesty that the man whom we rely on as Prime Minister is Petre Groza."

"The US and UK representatives asked me today who might be best to be appointed (as Prime Minister – D.C.G.). I told them that this is Your Majesty's responsibility and decision only. Therefore I did not tell them about the issue and I make it known to Your Majesty as a recommendation. Your Majesty has the sovereignty, whereas the morality is on your side."[4]

As it often happens, the harder the problem, the deeper the cynicism.

There was no choice left either for the King or the Prime Minister who resigned on February 28. It is noteworthy that the National Democratic Front ministers did not want to withdraw from the Cabinet but insisted that the premier resign. Nominally General Rădescu stayed in office pending consultations with party leaders and Soviet officials.

The political crisis was not an ordinary one. For the first time in Romania's contemporary history a cabinet dismissal and a prime-minister nomination, were directly ordered by a foreign power.[5]

Rumors spread rife: it was said that the NDF was apparently considering Dr. Nicolae Lupu, a national peasant leader, as the new premier. The well known communist leader Ana Pauker was supposed to have personally spoken to Dr. N. Lupu to accept the nomination. Seemingly Dr. Lupu had turned down the offer feeling that his own National Peasant Party wouldn't have been fairly represented in the New Cabinet.[6]

The Soviet choice notwithstanding the King made a short lived attempt to secure a non partisan prime-minister. Both Prince Barbu Ştirbey and General Avramescu were thought likely candidates. Eventually Prince Ştirbey was requested by the King to form a new coalition cabinet including all major parties.

The National Peasants and the Liberals were favouring the nomination. A Manifesto of the National Liberal Party called for immediate elections to be held supervised by the three powers represented on the ACC.

Ştirbey started exploratory talks with party leaders. He failed to secure either the NDF collaboration or the Allied (Soviet) Control Commission's approval. On March 1, the designated premier notified the King and publicly announced that he had to give up.

Andrey Vishinsky was uncompromising and turned down any attempt of a coalition government similar to the previous ones with a non partisan premier.

On March 1 after Barbu Ştirbey had returned his mandate, King Mihai called on Dr. Petre Groza. The latter started discussions with party leaders and requested representatives of Bucharest newspapers to attend a press conference the same day at 7 p.m. The afternoon daily *Ultima Oră* printed that Dr. Petre Groza had been officially nominated by the King. The press conference was canceled since the King delayed his decision by 24 hours contrary to Groza's expectations.[7]

However on March 2, 1945, in view of the virtual Soviet ultimatum, King Mihai asked Dr. Petre Groza to form a New Cabinet. The mandate was pending the participation of the National Peasants and Liberals. Iuliu Maniu and Constantin I.C. (Dinu) Brătianu were informed by the King of the latest evolutions.

How did the traditional political parties react?

It seems that Iuliu Maniu initially dismissed the very idea of Petre Groza's designation as Premier. Maniu's opinion, the three allied who signed the Armistice Convention and the Crimea Declaration had to decide on the issue of a Romanian coalition government. There ought to be tripartite consensus and not an unilateral Soviet decision.

The leaders of the National Peasant and Liberal parties, and the public opinion at large considered the Yalta Declaration at its face value. This is why the first reaction was to fight for time and to try delaying tactics.

The National Peasant Party (NPP) issued a confidential statement distributed presumably in typed copies only. It focused on three points:

1. Mr. Maniu and the NPP reject a monochromatic NDF cabinet and the inclusion of Mr. Gh. Tătărescu "whom they accuse of having initiated fascism in Romania", (in retrospect the opinion appears biased and partisan – D.C.G.).

2. The only acceptable formula is a coalition government in which the National Peasants and the Liberals "should posses the same majority as today".

3. Mr. Maniu and his party "are firmly convinced that, if British and American representatives support the views expressed above under 1 and 2, the USSR authorities will surely renounce to obtain from His Majesty the King by exertion or threat, a decision to the contrary".[8]

Such views proved totally ineffectual.

Within days after the Crimean Conference it was clear that the same concepts or "democracy... democratic... representative... freedom... civic liberties... elections... people's will..." had completely different meanings to Washington DC. or London on one hand and to Kremlin on the other hand. According to *Grai Nou* the Bucharest daily of the Soviet Army, the main outcome of the Crimea meeting was to maintain allies' unity and "to wipe out fascism and nazism from the face of the earth". In the former axis satellites, democratic governments should not be "distorted by pro-nazis to the abuse for their own ends of democratic liberties and for the thwarting of the people's struggle against fascism and the reaction which is akin to it".[9]

Upon Vishinsky's arrival in Bucharest the National Democratic Front launched a new slander offensive against the traditional parties and the King's advisors. The controlled press repeatedly and vociferously stressed that only a NDF government of "real democratic forces" could save the country from "fascists" including Maniu and Brătianu.

Radio Moscow gave strong support to the NDF allegations. The Soviets later broadcast that General Rădescu gathered large military forces close to Bucharest and organized many illegal arms supply depots, thus preparing a new dictatorial regime. It was also alleged that several headquarters of the National Peasant Party were actually arms depots.[10]

On Mach 3, late in the evening or during the night, a band of 60 armed men attacked the printing plant of *Dreptatea*, the National Peasant Party daily. They smashed the plates ready to print the next day issue and illegally arrested several printers.[11]

Two weeks later 18 printers were still detained at the Bucharest Police Headquarters on the order of Teohari Georgescu the Communist Interior Minister. A US representative of the ACC succeeded in interviewing two printers from *Dreptatea*. They gave "physical evidence of maltreatment". They also confirmed their being detained by "civilian NDF partisans", adding that "all those arrested have been subjected to continuous mistreatment".[12]

Fear and confusion loomed over Bucharest. The Romanian *Siguranța*, i.e. information agency, and the Military Commander of the city expressed their inability to even investigate the aggression at the *Dreptatea* Printing Plant, as a consequence of the latest Soviet order to reduce all Romanian military units and structures. At the same time the

Military Commander of Bucharest reported 56 robberies in one night (March 3rd to 4th) with no adequate police personnel to enforce law and order.[13]

When Barbu Ştirbey failed to form a new cabinet, King Mihai told Iuliu Maniu that the only alternative left is to ask Petre Groza to form a coalition cabinet of all democratic parties and groups under conditions that were to be decided upon. The conversation took place on March 1, 1945.[14]

Iuliu Maniu and the NPP committee were of the opinion that the King should not ask the representative of the smallest political group (the Plowmen Front headed by Petre Groza a local district organization in the fall of 1944) to form the Cabinet. According to the 1923 Constitution the mandate should be given either to a representative of the most popular party or to a neutral personality able to rally a general support. Therefore the NPP suggested its vice president Dr. Nicolae Lupu as possible premier if the King had no preference for a non-partisan prime minister.[15]

King Mihai had no choice but to comply with A. Vishinsky's "recommendation".

Dr. Petre Groza resumed his discussion with all party leaders late evening March 2, 1945.

He met Iuliu Maniu.

Two opposed statements were made about the talk.

According to the National Democratic Front communiqué Dr. Petre Groza suggested to NPP and NLP "that they should name their representatives in the government" and were offered two or three places each. The offer was turned down by Iuliu Maniu, Dr. Nicolae Lupu, vice president of the NPP, and Dinu Brătianu, president of NLP.

However "members of the dissident fractions of these parties entered the government of concentration of democratic forces, formed by Dr. Petre Groza".[16]

The National Peasants (NPP) Communiqué gave a different version, according to which Petre Groza informed Iuliu Maniu that "he cannot offer the (National Peasant) Party to collaborate in the Government".

Groza suggested "that a few members of the National Peasant Party *whom personally approved of* should be in the government but *without portfolios*, only as observers" (my italics, D.C.G.). The permanent delegation, i.e. the governing body, of the NPP rejected the proposal on March 3, 1945, at 10 a.m.[17]

The communist NDF actually rejected the very idea of a coalition cabinet with the NPP and the Liberals. In Groza's interpretation members of the National Peasant and National Liberals parties were to be selected in their individual capacities and not as representatives of their parties. Such a move would have enabled the communists to claim that the NDF government includes all democratic forces as stated by the Yalta Declaration. All the communists needed in March 1945 was makeshift formula and not proper coalition government. The same formula but implemented to a lesser degree would be approved by the Soviets, US and UK ministers of Foreign Affairs at their meeting in Moscow in December 1945. It resulted into a "reshuffled" Groza government which was officially recognized by all three major powers. As for the ministers without portfolio their role was nil.

Notwithstanding the National Peasants' rebuttal, Dr. Petre Groza approached two NPP leaders, Emil Ghilezan and Aurel Leucuția, i.e. respectively undersecretary of finances and Minister of the National Economy in the Rădescu Government. Both told Groza that their answer would be decided upon by the permanent delegation of NPP.

The designated Premier also turned to Gheorghe Tătărescu, twice Prime Minister of King Carol II, 1934–1937 and 1939–1940, leader of a dissident National Liberal Group. The latter expressed his willingness to participate as vice premier provided his party keeps the ministers of Finance, Economy and War Supplies.[18]

Were ready to join any NDF cabinet, *The Union of Patriots*, *The Plowmen Front*, the Trade Unions (the *General Confederation of Labor*), the dissident *National Peasant*, and the Organization of the *Democratic Priests* all with a clear pro-communist orientation.

Thus on March 3, 1945, Petre Groza presented the King with a list of 21 ministers: twelve communists, including their subordinates, four dissident–liberals, two dissident national–peasants and three social–democrats, the latter strongly in favour of the communist party dominance.[19]

The key positions of the Interior, Information, Justice and Communications were held by known communist leaders.[20]

The King made a last attempt. He did not approve the tentative government and asked the designated premier to offer the traditional parties (the NLP and NPP) a genuine cooperation under conditions to be discussed.

At the same time the King appealed to the NPP leaders to accept an eventual NDF offer of collaboration pointing out the very difficult and threatening situation the country was in. The permanent delegation of the National Peasant Party decided to accept in principle to participate in the Groza government asking that the basic constitutional provisions were respected, especially the civil rights and freedoms, freedom of press, of labor, of meetings, as well as a correct functioning of the democratic institutions. The National Peasant Permanent Delegation also demanded the immediate enactment of an agrarian law as drafted by NPP.[21]

The National Peasant leaders felt compelled to formulate these basic demands since they knew that the communist lead coalition had a very peculiar and different view on the civil rights and liberties. The choices for the traditional parties were either to bow to the communist proposals or to fully reject them.

The King and the designated Premier Petre Groza were informed of the NPP decision.

No further steps were taken on March 4 and 5, 1945, since the Soviets and local communists were in no mood to compromise. Dinu Brătianu head of the National Liberal Party had an audience with King Mihai, prior of the Royal approval of the Groza Cabinet. Iuliu Maniu did not attend and sent no responsible party representative. This was viewed by local observers as a political move by Maniu to dissociate the National Peasant Party from Dinu Brătianu's advice. Brătianu allegedly urged the King not to abdicate at that time.[22]

Meanwhile Dr. Petre Groza made some retouches to his proposals with more drive to the left. On the March 3rd list, there were 21 ministers, 12 of whom (some 57 per cent) were communists and their affiliates. On the new list which eventually was approved by King Mihai there were 12 communist ministers (some 66.6 per cent) in a total of 18. The remaining 6 posts were divided evenly between the Social Democrats and the dissident liberals.

Two days after the Groza Government was in office, Iuliu Maniu told an US interviewer that the King had been forced to accept the new cabinet. The National Peasant leader reiterated that Romania's political situation was not a matter to be decided solely by the USSR. Maniu expressed his marked discontent with the British and US media for not reacting to the distorted news on Romania coming via Moscow. He considered Romania as virtually "lost to the Russians" and feared an eventual Soviet annexation. The elections held under the communist lead NDF would probably amount to the same result even if impartial observers were placed at the polling booths.[23]

There was, however a second Maniu–Groza brief meeting, on March 6, at 2 p.m. Dr. Groza said he was in hurry because of the workers' meeting planned in the *Piața Națiunii* (Nation's Plaza). He did not discuss the issues, said only that the National Liberals (Brătianu) did not accept to cooperate, and that in the new cabinet the National Democratic Front should get the majority including ministries of the Interior, of National Defense and Foreign Affairs.[24]

The workers' meeting Groza referred to had been scheduled by the NDF prior to the Royal approval of the new cabinet. Had the King delayed or refused to confirm the cabinet, the NDF would have forced its acceptance through a mass demonstration.[25]

The meeting took place on March 6, 1945, in the afternoon. People were brought in to gratefully cheer the NDF representatives and to boo and threaten all the "reactionaries" and the "fascists" headed by Maniu, Brătianu and Rădescu. The pro-communist press alleged that 800,000 persons attended the meeting. The real number couldn't exceed 50,000 since the Nation's Plaza couldn't accommodate more.[26]

In a statement to the press, on March 7, Prime Minister Dr. Petre Groza outlined the program of his government.[27] Groza included an indirect warning to the King as he stressed that "the will of the people has fortunately been heeded by the crown and we are happy that these two factors the people and the sovereign have met on the same road. How bad it would have been otherwise."[28]

The whole communist press claimed victory ascertaining that all opponents had been eliminated. An editorial of *Era Nouă* (New Era) of March 12, stressed that Iuliu Maniu had been virtually ousted from politics. In his egotism, the editorial continued, Maniu considered the Peasant Party as "the only democratic force in Romania". He sought to monopolize the political scene and constantly refused to associate with the NDF and the "popular will".[29]

Similar comments were published in *Scânteia* the daily communist and *România Liberă*.

The National Peasants reacted promptly despite the black out imposed by NDF government to the opposition. Groza's aim, stated a NPP communiqué,[30] was to pass off his monochromatic NDF cabinet as a coalition of democratic forces. This was achieved with "the participation of a few renegades of the last minute as was admitted even by the communiqué of the NDF council". Moreover, the National Democratic Front suppressed the freedom of the press by ordering workers not to print opposition papers and by illegally arresting printers.

After "the public forces" were disarmed, the NDF armed guards occupied public buildings. An all out libelous press campaign presented the National Peasant Party as reactionary and insincere toward "our great allies". The Groza Government was formed through hitherto unused pressure "on the crown itself which was thus confronted with the alternative of either accepting it or abdicating".

With all that in view, the National Peasant Party promised "to continue the struggle for freedom and democracy... in order to bring about the triumph of the *free will of the nation which does not accept this government whose ideology and methods are alien to the soul of the nation*". (my italics D.C.G.)[31]

The National Peasants Party communiqué could not be printed and was therefore multiplied and distributed by hand.

XII. BACK TO THE ALLIED (SOVIET) CONTROL COMMISSION ON THE LATEST DEVELOPMENTS

Whilst the communist take over of the Romanian Government was completed between February 28 and March 6, the Allied (Soviet) Control Commission met several times and discussed the events. The outcome was practically nil and the Soviet had it their way.

The first meeting took place on February 28, 1945, at 8 p.m., the very day when at Vishinsky's demand, Premier Rădescu was forced to resign. The talks lasted 50 minutes. Colonel General Ivan Zaharovitch Susaikov the new deputy chairman of ACC, General Vinogradov the outgoing Deputy Chairman, rear Admiral Bogdenko, Naval Aide to marshal Rodion Malinovski, Air vice Marshal Stevenson, British commissioner, Brigadier General C.V.R. Schuyler, chief US representative, Russian, British and United States liaison officers, interpreters and recorders were present. The purpose of the meeting was to introduce the new Deputy Chairman of the ACC, General Susaikov.

The chief US representative fully backed by the British commissioner submitted to the New Deputy Chairman four questions to be answered "at the earliest practicable moment", namely:

1. Did A. Vishinsky meet once or several times yesterday and today, 27 and 28 February, with King Mihai, and asked him to dismiss Premier Rădescu and his cabinet?

2. Did A. Vishinsky offer any suggestions for a new government?

3. If so, were these suggestions made in the name of ACC or of Soviet administration?

4. What are the reasons for the Soviets to proceed like this without prior consultation with the British and US representatives?[1]

UK Air vice marshal Stevenson informed General Susaikov of the content of a letter sent by the British political advisor in Romania to Andrey Vishinsky the same afternoon. "I have just received report" – the British representative wrote in his letter – "that a request has been made by you to His Majesty the King of Romania that His Majesty should publish a decree dismissing the Prime Minister, General Rădescu, by 6 p.m. today and that a successor should be nominalized by 8 p.m", (the letter is dated 5:30 p.m., 28 February 1945).

Therefore the British commissioner was asking whether "the report is in accordance with the facts. And if so whether this request is made in the name of USSR". If the answer is affirmative, then it seems that the Soviet Government wishes "to see altered the present constitutional procedure of this state (Romania). Since "such a question is of direct interest to His Majesty's Government (British Government) it would appear that it could only be made the subject of discussion with the Romanian Government after prior consultation with the other allied governments. I most earnestly inform you that unless such prior agreement has been secured, His Majesty's Government may wish publicly to dissociate themselves from this action."[2]

Furthermore the British commissioner requested a confirmation of a report that the Romanian military garrison of Bucharest had been ordered by the Soviet command to give up all automatic weapons now in their possession. Vice Air Marshal Stevenson asked for information regarding whether Romanian units were forbidden to move throughout the country "without specific authority from the Russian commanders". He also reminded the new Soviet Deputy Chairman of the ACC of UK letter protesting the closing of the National Liberal daily *Viitorul* and the general line of the Soviet censorship which prevents the traditional Romanian parties to publicly express their views.

General Susaikov's answers were noncommittal. He had just arrived and was not familiar with ACC problems. "He would be glad to meet at a later date and to discuss any questions which might be brought up." At the closing of the meeting he "reiterated his promise to study all the problems presented by the United States and British representatives and to provide a comprehensive answer thereto "*at some future date*" (my italics D.C.G.).[3]

The British ACC representative had sent a telegram to London that morning (February 28) with the following comments:

1. The actions of A. Vishinsky without prior consultation of all ACC representatives are "considered to be in violation of the Yalta decision".

2. "*...the present political situation in Romania is a direct result of the attitude and action of the Soviet authorities* over the past few months and is in fact the crucial phase of a long campaign directed toward the ultimate Sovietization of the Romanian State" (my italics D.C.G.).

3. Unless the British and US governments react strongly "Romania will now be forced to accept a regime which is almost entirely leftist and *which is repugnant to the vast majority of the people*". Once in power such a regime will carry out "the remaining steps necessary to complete the Sovietization of Romania". Brigadier General Schuyler informed Air Vice Marshal Stevenson that he "concurred in full" with his colleague's statements (my italics D.C.G.).[4]

Another ACC meeting took place on March 4, 1945, at 3 p.m., and was attended by Colonel General Susaikov, rear Admiral Bogdenko, and

Brigadier General Schuyler.[25] It was one day before the Groza government was officially announced. The US representative reminded his Soviet counterpart of the four questions submitted to A. Vishinsky on February 28, 1945. General Susaikov said that "these questions had been submitted yesterday to Mr. Vishinsky who answered that in his opinion they had already been fully covered in a discussion on March 1st between the US representative, Mr. Berry and Mr. Vishinsky". If the brigadier general Schuyler wanted more information, general Susaikov "would be glad to transmit any further questions desired".[6]

One issue raised during the talk revealed the US representative's authority within the Allied (Soviet) Control Commission . General Schuyler plane was in Italy and needed Soviet clearance to fly back. An air member of the US military mission in Romania lt. colonel Emmers had gone to Italy two weeks earlier and was unable to bring the plane back due to lack of clearance.

General Susaikov's reply was that all flights had been stopped in Romania "as a result of recent unsettled conditions". Once a new set of identifications signals are distributed "to all friendly pilots", the flights would be resumed. The Soviet Deputy Chairman agreed to dispatch a "personal telegram" to Marshal Rodion Malinovsky requesting the reentry authorization for the US plane. He asked the necessary data for clearance to be given to the Soviet air section.

Brigadier General Schuyler reminded his colleague that "all such data had been furnished to the Air Soviet section two weeks ago".

Three weeks later the US representative stressed in his report that the British and US delegations on the ACC "*are still observers only*". He added significantly: "*Practically no information is vouchsafed to us*, and that which we definitely request is given to us only in the most general terms... all my comments and recommendations were courteously received, but always with the same reply that they would be referred to Moscow for decision. *In no case was anything further done in the matter*"[7] (my italics D.C.G.)

At the same ACC meeting on March 4, 1945, Brigadier General Schuyler reminded Colonel General Susaikov that he was still waiting an answer to the problem of the Romanian home forces which had dramatically been reduced to the point of not being able to "insure internal security". For example, continued General Schuyler, the night before, i.e. March 3rd to 4th, 1945, 56 robberies had been committed, two persons killed and "60 persons broke into a newspaper office, destroyed machinery and kidnapped nine employees".

In General Susaikov's estimations the Romanian administration had enough forces to keep internal security namely 20,000 men at all classes including 2,225 police and gendarmes in and around Bucharest. He himself couldn't check all reported cases. But even if true, the situation was due to the "Romanian unwillingness" to maintain order. The Bucharest police "are all proper armed" and "sufficient arms are available to all units". He eventually said that "ever since the army had been radically reduced they had assumed a non-cooperative attitude" and the Soviets had to use strong measures "in order to persuade them to carry on properly".

General Susaikov outlined once again the two main reasons which enabled the ACC to intervene:

a) to maintain order in the rear of the front, and

b) to carry out "to the letter" the obligations stipulated by the Armistice Convention.

Exactly the same motivations were expressed by the local communists during the events of February 1945: Premier Rădescu and all "reactionaries" were inciting and pushing to "civil war", and there was no sincere and complete observance of the armistice terms.

"It must be remembered" concluded General Susaikov "that the allied representatives, ACC, had come to Romania not by invitation but as conquerors, that the Romanians should not be requested to meet their obligations but rather should be forced to do so". He added that "if the Romanians themselves cannot do this satisfactorily, the Allied Control Commission will show them how to do it". He proposed to take strong measures to eliminate the last vestiges of fascism and sabotage and he hoped that General Schuyler would support them.[8]

The Soviet Deputy Chairman of the ACC had diverted the discussion to the armistice terms. Everyone knew that Romania had lost the war and had to pay. The real issue was the Soviet willingness to impose a communist regime.

The third ACC meeting took place on March 5, at 3:30 p.m.[9]

As previously, the talks met a dead end. General Schuyler referred to a possible "coup d'état by one or more political parties" and requested the ACC to take steps. He mentioned very recent statements made by the designated premier to the King and political party leaders that if prompt decision is not taken for a NDF government then he, Dr. Petre Groza, could not be held accountable for the actions of his supporters who were eager to go on.

General Susaikov pointed out that NDF is not a party but a mix of "Romanian democratic parties" and therefore "represents the people of Romania". The Soviet Deputy Chairman went on with the well known communist assertions relentlessly repeated in the previous days. The

Rădescu government was not "truly representative of the people of Romania". It had taken "into itself" a lot of fascist and nazi sympathizers and put them at the top and "those fascists and nazis are doing everything in their power to sabotage the interests of the United Nations in Romania." General Susaikov repeated time and again the invented story on the Rădescu cabinet and the February events. Brigadier General Schuyler tried again to explain that the desire of the US administration is to see in Romanian a Government "which will be proportionately representative of all existing parties, including National Democratic Front parties, the National Peasant and National Liberal parties".

It was all in vain. Schuyler's words fell of deaf ears. His Soviet colleague was unyielding and told him that "*the people do not wish a government of Rădescu's type, that they are requesting a government which comprises the democratic elements*" (my italics D.C.G.). Thus the Soviet representative knew better than anyone what the Romanians wished. Again he stressed the need to keep order in the rear of the front line and concluded: "In view of the fact that the Rădescu Government did not seem to be able to maintain control in Romania and preserve order, *the type of (Rădescu) Government cannot be expected to remain in Romania* or to be upheld. *It does not represent the will of the people*" (my italics D.C.G.). In order to give more weight to his opinions, General Susaikov warned his US colleague "not to take too close" to his heart the information that the Romanians may give you. "The Romanians are ready to get every little bit of misleading information possible, blow it up into a big balloon and let then everything explode as a provocation against the Soviets." No examples were given.

Then General Susaikov pointed out again the imbalance between Romanian troops at the front and in the rear. The figures were almost the same as stated by the Soviets at the ACC meeting of February 20, 1945. However one figure was different. The previous day Colonel General Susaikov had said that 20,000 men were in and around Bucharest. Twenty four hours later and with Rădescu no longer Prime Minister, the same Soviet Deputy Chairman of the Allied Control Commission declared: "in Bucharest there are 52,000 military personnel. That shows that they do not have a mutual desire to fight the Germans. They just want to pass the time; later on they will be able to say that they participated in this fight."[10]

The report on the ACC meetings reached the State Department some 17–18 days later.[11]

The Pentagon and the State Department were regularly kept informed about the developments. On February 28 Burton Berry, the US political representative, cabled about the meeting previous evening between the

King, Constantin Vişoianu and Andrey Vishinsky.[12] On March 1, Berry announced that Rădescu was forced to resign "in accordance with the demand of Vishinsky".[13] On March 3, 1945, General Schuyler informed the Pentagon and State Department that "Vishinsky has confirmed to the King Mihai of Romania, that a government headed by Groza will be acceptable to the Soviet authorities."[14]

Thus the real meaning of the events was known.

The discussions within the ACC could not change the communist drive to full power. The tripartite Yalta Declaration on liberated Europe was loose enough in its wording to give way to any interpretation.

XIII. WINSTON CHURCHILL, FRANKLIN DELANO ROOSEVELT AND ANDREY VISHINSKY ON THE FEBRUARY EVENTS IN ROMANIA

In London and Washington DC. real politics prevailed over general principles and declarations. On March 8, forty eight hours after the imposition of the Groza Government in Romania, Prime Minister Winston Churchill sent a "personal and top secret" telegram to president Franklin Delano Roosevelt. The excerpts are self explanatory: "I fell sure that you will be as distressed as I am by recent events in Romania. The Russians have succeeded in establishing the rule of a communist minority by force and misrepresentation. We have been hampered in our protest against these developments by the fact that, in order to have freedom to save Greece, Mr. Eden and I at Moscow in October recognized that Russia should have largely preponderant voice in Romania and Bulgaria while we took the lead in Greece. Stalin adhered very strictly to this understanding during the thirty days' fighting against communists and ELAS in the city of Athens, in spite of the fact that all this was most disagreeable to him and those around him..."

"...Stalin is now pursuing the opposite course in the two Black Sea Balkan countries (i.e. Romania and Bulgaria – D.C.G.) and one which is absolutely contrary to all democratic ideas. Since the October Anglo–Russian conversations in Moscow, Stalin has subscribed on paper to the principles of Yalta which are certainly being trampled down in Romania."

"Nevertheless I am most anxious not to press this view to such an extent that Stalin will say 'I did not interfere with your action in Greece why do you not give me the same latitude in Romania?' This again would lead to comparisons between the aims of his action and those of ours. On this neither side would convince the other. Having regard to my personal relations with Stalin, I am sure it would be a mistake for me at this stage to embark in the argument."

Was there anything to be done in these circumstances?

Winston Churchill put forward two proposals: "...I feel that he (Stalin) should be informed of out distress at developments which led to the setting up by force of a Government in Romania of a communist minority since this conflicts with conclusions of Declaration on Liberated Europe upon which we were agreed at Crimea Conference." Stalin was most likely not impressed or affected by Winston Churchill's distress.

The second proposal focused on possible early communist reprisals: "...more especially I am afraid that the advent of this Communist Government may lead to an indiscriminate purge of the anticommunist Romanians who will be accused of fascism much on the lines of what has been happening in Bulgaria".

Was any action considered?

"I would suggest therefore that Stalin should be asked to see to it that the new government *does not immediately start a purge of all political elements which are in opposition to their views* on grounds that they have been encouraged to do so by the Yalta Declaration" (my italics D.C.G.).

Winston Churchill concluded: "...I should be grateful to know your views. Pray let this telegram be between you and me."[1]

The mass arrests and political trials in Romania started July–August 1947. It is unknown whether Winston Churchill's fears of an immediate purge postponed extended political arrests in Romania till July–August 1947. It seems more likely that the need to fully implement and to strengthen the control over the country lead the Romanian Communist Party to delay the enmass political repression.

President Franklin Delano Roosevelt speedily answered on March 11, 1945.[2] He told Winston Churchill to have "very much in mind the considerations with regard to Romania and to the Polish question" raised by the British premier's telegram. "I am fully determined, as I know you are, not to let the good decisions we reached at the Crimea slip through our hands and will certainly do everything I can to hold Stalin to their honest fulfillment."

Announcing that he has instructed US Ambassador in Moscow to take up the whole question with Molotov, the US President continued: "It is obvious that the Russians have installed a minority government of their choosing, but apart from the reasons you mentioned in your message, *Romania is not a good place for a test case* (my italics D.C.G.). There were two reasons for that: 1. The Russians have been in undisputed control from the beginning, and 2. With Romania lying athwart the Russian lines of communications it is moreover difficult to contest the plea of military necessity and security which they are using to justify their action."

The conclusion: "We shall certainly do everything we can, however, and of course will count on your support."[3]

There was in fact almost nothing President Roosevelt could have dome with regard to the whole East-European area in March 1945. From Poland to Bulgaria the Soviets were in full control and the Western Allies had nothing but general declarations at disposal. Furthermore F.D. Roosevelt gave apparently complete credit to the Soviet "motivation" for ousting Rădescu's Government, namely the need to secure the rear front communication lines in Romania.

Throughout 1945, there will be much talking between the three war allies on the procommunist regimes installed by the Soviets in Romania and Bulgaria. In the case of the former the outcome will eventually be to accept the communist take over of the government completed on March 6, 1945.

The writing of an invented sequence of events by the Romanian procommunist and Soviet media had started in February 1945 as the developments unfolded. This version was imposed for decades with no possibility to unveil the truth.

One of the staunch promoters of the invented history was Andrey Vishinsky himself.

In a letter with regard to the situation in Romania and sent to the Soviet Government on September 1, 1945, the United States Government reminded the imposition of the Groza Cabinet at the insistence of the Soviet Deputy People's Commissar for Foreign Affairs.

Three days later in his reply note Vishinsky made the following comment: The United States intervention "...makes clear the inadmissibility to the Soviet Union of your proposal regarding the resignation of the *Government of Petre Groza which was formed* by no means at the insistence of the Assistant People's Commissar for Foreign Affairs of the USSR as you write, but as *the result of the union of the democratic forces of the country*, (my italics D.C.G.) and this has been demonstrated by the half year of existence of the present Romanian Government, which enjoys the full support of the majority of the Romanian people."[4] Vishinsky continued by throwing the blame for the Romanian developments on US and UK representatives of the Allied Control Commission in Bucharest.

A. Harriman the US ambassador in Moscow met A. Vishinsky on September 12, 1945, and took the occasion "to reproach him in a friendly manner" for sending the state department a note "such as the last we have received on the Romanian question"...[5]

The imposition of Dr. Petre Groza government had a follow-up. General Nicolae Rădescu requested and was granted sanctuary at the British Mission in Bucharest in the evening of March 5. He presented evidence that his life was in danger. Air Vice Marshal Stevenson who acted on authority from London informed "at once" the ACC Soviet Deputy Chairman of the action. Colonel General Susaikov replied promptly: "Your letter of the 6th March 1945 under no. 429 has very much surprised me in as much as the control of order and safety in Romania is carried out by the ACC under the direction of the Soviet High Command. Under these circumstances your actions appear incorrect and the whole responsibility for them must rest on you... Communication had been passed to the Romanian Government."[6]

Air Vice Marshal Stevenson informed his US colleague that he had similar authority to grant sanctuary "if need rises" to King Mihai, the Queen Mother and Iuliu Maniu. Brigadier General C.V.R. Schuyler was requested to participate in this action. He did not so pending on new instructions from the War and State Departments.[7]

Did Iuliu Maniu make any attempt to get in touch with the US representatives in Bucharest during the last phase of the February–March crisis? The answer seems to be no. Neither Iuliu Maniu or any of his authorized representatives ever asked to see anyone from the US Mission to find out the attitude of the American administration regarding the situation in Romania. Maniu, however sent "the wife of one of his friends, a lady of no political experience" to the British political representative.[8] One has to admit in retrospect that however well and precisely informed, nobody could have changed the course of events in Romania as planned and implement by the Soviets and their local communist subordinates in February–March 1945.

One more question: to what extent did the US and UK representatives with the Allied Control Commission in Bucharest know what prevailed with the decision makers in Washington DC. and London? It seems that the US and British representatives tried earnestly to avoid the imposition of the communist lead minority government in Romania. Yet, after March 6, 1945, were they informed by their officials that things had to be accepted as they were? For over two and half years until November 1947, Washington and London periodically protested against the events which lead to complete communist regime in Romania. Each time the Western notes were flatly rejected by the Groza government fully backed by the Soviets.

ENDNOTES

Introduction

1. Memorandum of the British Embassy in Washington to the State Department, dated February 8, 1944; 871.00/1008, National Archives, Washington DC.

2. *Idem*, § 8.

3. *Idem*, § 9.

4. Memorandum by the US State Department for Admiral Leahy on February 11, 1944: 871.00/1008, National Archives, Washington DC.

5. *Ibidem*.

6. The Memo of the Joint Chiefs of Staff to the State Department is signed by Admiral William D. Leahy and is dated February 29, 1944: 871.00/1010, National Archives, Washington DC.

7. *Ibidem*. Admiral William Leahy added that it was "essential that Russia should be kept informed of the progress of any such undertakings".

8. Telegram no. 3121, August 23, 1944, at 9 p.m., from Moscow to the Secretary of State Washington DC: 740.00119 E.W./8–2344, National Archives, Washington DC. The Soviet official on August 23 was the Acting Chief of the American Division of the Soviet Foreign Office.

9. Foreign Relations of the United States. Diplomatic Papers (FRUS) 1944, Volume IV, Europe, Washington DC, 1966, p. 192. Telegram no. 3135, from Moscow at 5 p.m. 749.00119 E.W./8–2444.

10. Telegram no. 3147, August 25, at 3 a.m. From Moscow to the Secretary of State, Washington DC: FRUS, IV, p. 193 (740.00119 E.W./8–2544).

11. FRUS, IV, pp. 193–238.

12. King Mihai sent a Memorandum to President Franklin Delano Roosevelt on January 24, 1945 with the analysis of the situation in Romania, some five months after the military coup. The memo estimates that *more than 150,000 soldiers* were interned in camps by the Soviets starting August 24, 1944: 871.00/3–545.

13. FRUS, IV, 1944, p. 193, telegram 3148 sent by US Ambassador Harriman from Moscow, on August 25, 1944.

14. The royal decree no. 1626 of August 31, 1944, published in the *Monitorul Oficial* (The Official Gazette), no. 202 of September 2, 1944.

15. Eleodor Focşeneanu, *Istoria constituţională a României, 1856–1991* (The Constitutional History of Romania, 1856–1991), Humanitas, Bucharest 1992, pp. 88–90. Cf. Mihai T. Oroveanu, *Istoria dreptului românesc şi evoluţia instituţiilor constituţionale* (The History of the Romanian Law and the Evolution of the Constitutional Institutions), Cerma Publishing House, Bucharest, 1992, pp. 294–295.

16. Telegram no. 3382 from Ambassador A. Harriman in Moscow to the State Department, on September 8, 1944. The Armistice convention and the additional protocol for the establishment of the Allied Control Commission were signed on September 12: FRUS, IV, 1944, pp.225–226 and 232. For the two texts: Department of State *Bulletin*, September 17, 1944, pp. 289–292.

17. Robert R. King, *History of the Romanian Communist Party*, Hoover Institution Press, Stanford University, 1980, table 2, p. 64.

18. The Commission for the United Union Movement included six communists among them leaders Gheorghiu Dej, Chivu Stoica and Gheorghe Apostol, and five social democrats. The Unions were based on the principle of the unity of the working class, and on the principle of class–struggle: *România Liberă*, II, no. 23, Thursday September 7, 1944, p. 2.

19. *România Liberă*, II, no. 42, Tuesday September 26, 1944, p. 3.

20. *Idem*, p. 1.

21. For example see articles and notes in *România Liberă*, II, no. 50, October 4, 1944; then October 6, 15 (p. 1), 19 (p. 1), 21, 22, 29, 30 (p. 1 and 4), November 1, 4 etc. The communist daily *Scânteia* printed such news and aggressive comments every day.

22. *R.L.*, II, no. 48, October 2, 1944, p. 1 and 3; no. 45, September 29, 1944, p. 7; no. 47, October 1, 1944, p. 3 (for the Patriots' Union and the Popular Peasant Party); no. 52 October 6, 1944 (for the United Workers' Front); no. 49, October 3, (for the National Democratic Front of the Youth); no. 59, October 13, 1944 (for the Democratic University Students).

23. According to the pro-communist press there were tens of thousands of participants. There is no possibility to check such assertions. More likely the NDF supporters paraded by the thousands on the Bucharest streets.

24. Over 75 per cent of the Romania's population lived in the rural areas and was fundamentally hostile to the communist collectivization.

25. NDF meetings took place in all major towns. The pro-communist press claimed that 100,000 participants attended a meeting at the ANEF Stadium. The Stadium had a maximum of 25,000 sitting and standing places. For the meeting see: *R.L.*, II, no. 67, Saturday, October 21, 1944. Meetings took place in Constanța (*R.L.* no. 64, Wednesday, October, 18, p. 6); Brașov, Galați, Craiova, Moreni (*R.L.*, no. 72, Thursday October 26, p. 3); at the Bucharest Railway station (*R.L.*, no. 70, Tuesday October 24, pp. 1 and 4); Ploiești, Timișoara, Câmpulung etc. (*R.L.* no. 71, Wednesday October 25, pp. 1 and 4).

26. R.L., II, no. 54. Thursday Oct. 19, 1944, p. 1.

27. R.L., II, no. 68, Sunday Oct. 22, 1944, p. 1 and 3.

28. *Dreptatea*, the official daily of the National Peasant Party, S2, I, Wednesday October 4, 1944, editorial by N. Carandino; *idem*, S2, I, no. 39, Monday October 9, 1944, interview by NPP president Iuliu Maniu.

29. *Dreptatea*, S. 2, I, no. 44, Sunday October 15, 1944, p. 1.

30. *Idem*, S. 2, I, no. 45, Monday Oct. 16, 1944, pp. 3–4.

31. *Dreptatea*, S. 2, I, no. 44, Sunday Oct. 15, p. 3 and no. 46, Wednesday Oct. 18, 1944, p. 3. There is no word about the Soviet intervention. The government had, however, absolutely no reason to stop the NPP meeting which was planned at the Scala Theater of Bucharest. The only explanation for the interdiction is the intervention of the Allied (Soviet) Control Commission. The OSS report from Bucharest and send through Caserta to Washington DC, dated October 29, 1944, gives details on the Romanian government's meeting on October 17, 1944. Iuliu Maniu and Constantin I.C. Brătianu pointed on that the NPP meeting on October 15, was suppressed at the request of the general V.P. Vinogradov, Soviet Deputy Chairman of the Allied (Soviet) Control Commission.

32. Pro-NPP meetings and rallies in the county of Maramureş, in Buzău, in Ţăndărei (Ialomiţa county), Braşov, etc. *Dreptatea* S. 2, I, no. 54, Friday Oct. 27, 1944, p. 4.

33. *Dreptatea* S. 2, I, no. 58, Wednesday, November 1, 1944, p. 4.

34. Telegram no. 1164, Kirk from Caserta to the State Department, on November 5, 1944, p. 1–2: National Archives (N.A.), Washington DC.

35. *Idem*, p. 2–3.

36. *Idem*. Iuliu Maniu had been previously prime-minister (Nov. 1928 to June 1930).

37. *Idem*.

38. On October 9, 1944 in Moscow: W. Churchill, *Triumph and Tragedy*, Bentham Books, New York, 1962, pp. 196–197.

39. *R.L.*, II, no. 83, Monday Nov. 6, 1944, p. 1.

40. Details in *R.L.*, II, no. 82, Sunday Nov. 5, 1944, p. 3; no. 88, Saturday Nov. 11, p. 3; no. 94, Friday Nov. 17, 1944, p. 3; no. 91, Tuesday Nov. 14, p. 5; no. 93, Thursday Nov. 16, p. 3; no. 99 Thursday Nov. 23, p. 3; no. 105 Nov. 30, p. 3; no. 106, Friday, December 1, 1944, pp. 1 and 3.

41. *R.L.*, II, no. 104, Wednesday Nov. 29, 1944, pp. 1–2 with five anti-NPP articles; no. 105, Thursday Nov. 30.

42. *R.L.* II, no. 100, Friday Nov. 24, 1944, p. 1; no. 101, Saturday Nov. 25, p. 3; no. 102, Sunday Nov. 26, p. 1; no. 103, Monday, Nov. 27, 1944, pp. 1 and 3.

43. *Idem*, p. 1–2. The Interior Minister in the Sănătescu government was Nicolae Penescu, general secretary of the National Peasant Party.

44. *R.L.*, II, no. 105, Thursday Nov. 30, 1944, p. 3.

45. A detailed account on Vyshinsky's activities in Romania, see Liliana Saiu, *The Great Powers and Romania, 1945–1946. A Study of the early Cold War era*, East Europeans Monographs, No. CCCXXXV, Boulder, 1992, p. 53–72.

46. *Idem*, p. 65. For Vishinsky's arrival in Bucharest: *R.L.*, II, no. 84, Friday Nov. 10, 1944, p. 8.

47. Telegram no. 25 of Nov. 24, 1944, Burton Berry from Bucharest to the Secretary of State: 871.00/11–2444, National Archives, Washington DC. Liliana Saiu, *Op. cit.*, p. 67: The Soviet notified on the troops' arrival on November 15, 1944.

48. The article provided for transit rights to be given to Soviet troops: telegram no. 25 of Nov. 24, 1944.

49. Telegram no. 35 of November 28, 1944, Burton Berry from Bucharest to the Secretary of State: 871.00/11–2844, National Archives, Washington DC, p. 3.

50. *Idem*, p. 1.

51. *Idem*, p. 1–2. The Soviet order for the withdrawal of the Romanian administration from Northern Transylvania in *R.L.*, II, no. 92, Wednesday Nov. 15, 1944, p. 1. See also *R.L.*, II, no. 89 Nov. 12, p. 1; no. 90 Nov. 13, p. 1; no. 93 Nov. 16, p. 3 (2 articles). See also telegram no. 37 of November 29, 1944, Burton Berry from Bucharest to the Secretary of State in FRUS, IV, 1944, pp. 269–270.

52. *R.L.* II, no. 109, Monday December 3, 1944, p. 3.

53. Telegram no. 35 of November 28, 1944, see footnote no. 49. Also telegram no. 40 of November 30 in FRUS, IV, 1944, pp. 270–271; Cf. Liliana Saiu, *Op. cit.*, pp. 68–69.

54. The merger of the handful member of the Ralea's Socialist-Peasant Party with the Petre Groza's Ploughmen Front was announced by the press on December 2, 1944; *R.L.*, II, no. 107, Friday December 2.

55. Telegram no. 1743, December 13, 1944, Kirk from Caserta to the Secretary of State: 871.01/12–1344, National Archives, Washington DC.

56. For the diplomatic components of the Romanian developments: Dr. Paul Quinlan, *Clash over Romania, British and American Policies toward Romania: 1938–1947*, Los Angeles, 1977; Liliana Saiu, *Op. cit.*. Saiu's volume include a detailed bibliography on the diplomatic aspects of the topic at pages 271–281.

Chapter I: The Rădescu Cabinet

1. See *Monitorul Oficial* (the Official Bulletin, *MO*) No. 238 bis, Wednesday December 6, 1944, pp. 7957–7958. The National Liberal and the National Peasant parties ruled often alternatively between 1919 and 1937, the former for eight years, the latter for three.
   The National Democratic Front was an ad-hoc coalition set up by the Communist Party in September 1944, and included: The Social Democrats, the only left wing party with popular support at that time; the Patriots' Union a communist organization to attract middle class citizens; the Ploughmen Front a small peasant organization at the Hunedoara county level, headed by Dr. Petre Groza; the Socialist Peasants' Party representing professor Mihai Ralea and a handful supporters only; the Trade Unions where the communists tried hard to get full control.
   In December 1944 the Communist Party of Romania had a few thousand registered numbers, then unable to seize directly the control of the country. This is why the NDF screen was much needed.

2. Neutral politically.

3. Report on the *Development of the Political Situation in Romania, December 1944 – January 1945*, London, March 5, 1945,

871.00/3–545 Department of State Archives, National Archives, Washington DC. See Annexes.

4. Same *Report*, p. 2.

5. Winston Churchill, *Triumph and Tragedy*, Vol. 6, Bantam Books, N.Y. 1962, Chapter 19: *Christmas at Athens*, pp. 264–279.

6. For example the daily pro-communist *România Liberă* did not carry out any attack on the National Peasant and Liberal leaders till the end of December 1944.

7. See *România Liberă (R.L.)*, II, 113, Saturday December 9, 1944, p.3. For the comments of the pro-communist press, *ibidem*, and *R.L.*, II, 114 Sunday December 10, 1944, p. 1. The editorial by N. Moraru reminded the need of a large and all encompassing purge and praised the mass actions which led to the change of county prefects and mayors. By this way, the editorial rejected some of the Premier Minister's demands.

8. The imposition of chief counties (prefects in Romanian) and town and village mayors was carried out by the communists through *popular assemblies* and local demonstrations with no proper ballot. The changes started in November 1944 and pro-communist *prefecţi* were forcibly appointed in the counties of Constanţa, Brăila, Arad, Prahova and Dîmboviţa all in the month of November. New mayors were imposed in the cities of Constanţa, Griviţa (Romanaţi), Brăila, Arad, Ploieşti and Tîrgovişte: *R.L.*, II, no. 105, Thursday November 30, 1944, p. 3; *R.L.*, II, no. 82, Sunday November 5, p. 3; *R.L.*, II, no. 94, Friday November 17, p. 3; no. 91, Tuesday November 14, p. 5; no. 93, Thursday November 16, p. 3; no. 99, Thursday November 23, p. 3. Once in charge, the new chiefs nominated the mayors of the other towns and of villages, all selected among the National Democratic Front members. No agreement could be reached between the NDF and the National Peasants and Liberals on the nominations to these offices.

9. Law no. 21 published in the *Monitorul Oficial*, vol. CXIII, no. 11, January 15, 1945, p. 227.

10. As county chiefs – as in Botoşani, Cîmpulung, Covurlui, Roman, Tecuci, Tutova and Prahova – and mayors. See: *M.O.*, vol. CXIII, no.

5, January 8, 1945, p. 83; also *M.O.*, no. 15, January 19, 1945, p. 374 and *M.O.* January 23, 1945, pp. 465–466.

11. Law no. 7, in *M.O.*, vol. CXIII, no. 2, Part I, January 5, 1945, pp. 64–65.

12. In *M.O.*, vol. CXIII, no. 30, Part I, February 7, 1945, pp. 819–821.

13. Articles 1 and 5 of the law on ethnic minorities.

14. *Idem*, articles 8–9, 10–11, 11–12, 15–16.

15. *Idem*, articles 18–22.

16. The officers were dismissed in 1940 for their Jewish background. (law no. 873, in *M.O.* 287/1940) The names of the reintegrated officers in *M.O.*, vol. CXIII, no. 10, Part I, January 13, 1945, pp. 187–205.

17. Law no. 67 of January 31, 1945, in *M.O.*, vol. CXIII, no. 26, Part I, February 2, 1945, pp. 708–709.

18. The enactment of the law was requested by the Armistice Convention signed in Romania with the USSR, USA, UK, in Moscow, on September 12, 1944.

19. Law no. 50 of January 20, 1945, in *M.O.*, vol. CXIII, no. 17, Part I, January 21, 1945, pp. 415–418.

20. *Idem*, pp. 418–419

21. As for example: Dumitru Săracu, Alexandrina Sidorovici, Constanţa Crăciun, Avram Bunaciu, Emilian Angheliu, Zaharia Tănase; in *M.O.*, vol. CXIII, no. 31, Part I, Fenbruary 8, 1945, p. 871 (decrees 319 and 320), and *idem*, no. 34, February 12, 1945, p. 968 (decree no. 388 of the Ministry of Justice).

22. Law no. 18, in *M.O.*, vol. CXIII, no. 8, Part I, January 11, 1945, p. 144.

23. *M.O.*, vol. CXIII, no. 25, Part I, February 1, 1945, p. 667, decree no. 62 of January 31st.

24. A *Commission for the organization of the United Trade Union Movement* with representatives of the Communist Party of Romania and the Social Democratic Party started its work on September 1, 1944. See *România Liberă*, II, no. 23, Thursday September 7, 1944, p. 2.

25. The law for the organization of the Trade Unions in *M.O.* See also Schuyler's *Report*, see footnote no. 36.

26. The Memo divided into 11 chapters was forwarded to President Franklin Roosevelt by William J. Donovan, director of the Office of Strategic Services (OSS) on March 5, 1945, National Archives, Washington DC, 871.00/3–545. The document has 40 doubled spaced typed pages and a letter of King Mihai to the US President.

27. Up to here is the content of Chapters I to III.

28. Chapter IV of the *Memoir* explains in detail the very negative consequences of the ACC decision.

29. Chapter VI of the *Memoir*. See also the reply of the ACC to the objection raised by the Romanian Armistice Commission, on December 3, 1944: in daily *Cotidianul*, no. 146, November 29, 1991, p. 5.

30. The German settled in Transylvania in the second half of the 12th century and in the Banat province in the 18th century.

31. Chapter VII of the *Memoir*.

32. Chapter VIII of the same *Memoir*.

33. Chapter IX of the same *Memoir*: the railway system had been partially widened to Russian gauge; Soviet personnel has replaced to a great extent the Romanian transport staff; about 12,500 railways cars and 140 steam engines have been sent outside the country's border; the stock of coal needed for the Romanian traffic had been dramatically reduced.

34. Chapter IX of the *Memoir*, pt.7.

35. Romanian translation of the Stettinius' telegram to the US representative at Bucharest, in the magazine *Expres Magazin* no. 2, Bucharest, August 8, 1990, p. 4.

36. War Department Archives, OPD 336 TS. The Report has 13 typed pages divided into : Air section; the Military situation; Political developments; Romania's economy.

37. *Idem*, Romania's economy, pt. 2.

38. *Idem*, Romanian's economy, pt. 3.

39. *Idem*, Romania's economy, pt. 7.

40. *Idem*, Romania's economy, pt. 8. The ACC note was dated February 6, 1945.

41. *Ibidem*.

42. *Idem*, the *Military situation in Romania*, pt. d and e. The lists with Romanian citizens of German ethnic background were published in *M.O.* vol. CXIII, no. 41, Part I, February 20, 1945, p. 1214 to 1292. At the meeting of the ACC in Bucharest, the Soviet Admiral Bogdenko confirmed that *approximately 80,000* Romanian–Germans were *mobilized* out of which 11,000 were work exempt by special report of the Romanian government and the remaining 69,000 have been sent to Russia: *Resume of the Conference 14 February (1945)*, 871.00/3.–845, State Department N.A. Washington DC, p. 1.

43. Same *Report, Romanian economy*, pt. 10 (see footnote no. 36)

44. Law no. 126, in *M.O.* vol CXIII, no. 45, Part I, February 24, 1945, p. 1433.

45. Decree–law no. 10 in *M.O.* vol. CXIII, no. 7, Part I, January 10, 1945, p. 122–123.

46. Report on the *Development of the Political situation in Romania December 1944 – January 1945*, London, March 5, 1945: 871.00/3–545, Department of State, National Archives (N.A.), Washington DC, p. 3 and 5.

47. There are no data to check the accuracy of these figures: *idem*, p. 4.

Chapter II: The End of a Three Weeks Political Truce

1. Text of the appeal in *România Liberă*, III, no. 131, Monday January 1, 1945, p. 6.

2. *Report*, p. 6–7 and 8.

3. *Idem*, p. 8.

4. *România Liberă*, III, no. 132, Thursday January 4, 1945, p. 1.

5. Same daily, III, no. 143, Thursday January 18, 1945, p. 1 and 3. In Ploieşti, Dej was greeted by Emil Bodnăraş, Petre Constantinescu-Iaşi, Iosif Rangheţ and general Vasiliu Răşcanu (supposedly independent high-ranking officer) whilst at Bucharest North railway station, Dej was welcomed by Ana Pauker, Vasile (Laszlo) Luca, and Teohari Georgescu.

6. The press conference took place on January 20, 1945; see *România Liberă*, III, no. 147, Monday January 22, 1945, p. 5. Dej went into some figures of the transportation agreement. He said for example that the Soviet government had accepted to postpone by two years the debiting of 2,200 railroad cars and 310 locomotives to the $300 million war reparations account as provided by the Armistice Convention.

7. *Ibidem*.

8. Some examples: *The outcome of Mr. Maniu policy*, by Grigore Preoteasa, in *România Liberă*, III, no. 133, Friday January 5, 1945, p. 1 and 3; *Mr. Maniu and the dissensions within the National Peasant Party* by Grigore Preoteasa, *idem*, no. 134, January 6, 1945; *Mr. Vaida Voevod and the dissensions within the National Peasant Party* by Grigore Preoteasa, *idem*, no. 137, Thursday January 11, 1945, p. 1. Preoteasa was the chief editor of the procommunist daily.

9. See supra, Chapter I and footnote no. 43.

10. Telegram no. 59 of January 23, 1945 by Burton Berry to the Secretary of State, 871.00B/1–2345, State Department, N.A.

11. Telegram no. 81, January 30, 1945, 871.00/1–3045, *ibidem*.

12. Telegram no. 59 of January 23, 1945.

13. *Ibidem*.

14. *Ibidem*.

15. See *Report*, p. 6 (footnote no. 2).

16. Telegram no. 1164 of November 5, 1944 Kirk from Caserta to the State Department, 871.01/12–1344, State Dept., N.A.

17. *Ibidem*.

18. *Report*, p. 9 (footnote no. 2)

19. Telegram no. 59 of January 23, 1945 (footnote no. 10).

20. Telegram no. 61 of January 24, 1945, 871.00B/1–2445, State Dept., N.A. Gheorghiu Dej spoke on January 22nd.

21. The September 1944 Program of the National Democratic Front (NDF) requested "the nationalization of the National Bank, of another 18 banks and of the basic industries".: *R.L.* II, no. 42, Tuesday, September 26, 1944, p. 1.

22. Telegram no. 62, January 26, 1945: 871.00B/1–2645, State Dept., N.A.

23. *Ibidem*.

24. Telegram no. 81, January 30, 1945: 871.00B/1–3045, State Dept., N.A.

Chapter III: The Begining of a New Political Crisis

1. Text in *România Liberă*, III, no. 153, Monday January 29, 1945, p. 3. In 1945–1946 the newspapers were antedated.

2. *Ibidem.*

3. Interview in *România Liberă*, III, no. 155, Thursday, February 1, 1945, p. 3.

4. *Ibidem.*

5. *Scânteia* the daily of the Communist Party, *România Liberă*, *Libertatea* of the Social Democratic Party (though to a lesser extent), *Frontul Plugarilor* of Dr. Petre Groza etc. printed every day attacks against the National Peasants and Liberals.

6. As for example: "The guarantee to a cobelligerency status: a NDF government", editorial by N. Moraru in *România Liberă*, III, no. 158, Sunday February 4, 1945, p. 1 and 3; "Romanian war prisoners in USSR," *Idem*, no. 156, Friday, February 2, 1945, p. 1 and 2; "When will the Romanian war prisoners return from USSR", by Tini Dumitrescu, *idem*, no. 157, Saturday February 4, 1945, p. 1 and 3; "Waiting for the war prisoners", by Mihai Apostolescu, *idem*, no. 165, Monday February 12, 1945, p. 1 and 2.

7. *România Liberă*, III, no. 155, Thursday February 1, 1945, p. 1.

8. See *România Liberă*, III, no. 159, February 5, 1945, p. 3 and 5; no. 160. 167, 169 etc. Same news in the other pro-communist newspapers.

9. *România Liberă*, III, no. 161, February 8, 1945. The purge would result in the control of the police by the communist party.

10. *România Liberă*, III, no. 166, 167, 168, 169, 170, February 12 through 18, 1945; also no. 175 February 24, 1945, p. 3; no. 180, March 1, p. 6; no. 181, March 2, p. 3.

11. A note published in *Ardealul*, V, no. 235, Saturday February 3, 1945, p. 3.

12. Statement of the Communist Committee of the Printers' Union: in *România Liberă*, III, no. 158, Sunday, February 4, 1945, p. 2.

13. The official daily of the Communist Party.

Chapter IV: Premier Rădescu's February 11, 1945 Speech at the Aro Theatre

1. Telegram no. 111, February 12, 1945: 871.00/2–1245, 08/EG, State Department, N.A.

2. *Idem*, p. 2.

3. An English translation of Rădescu's speech is in the State Dept. Archives following telegram no. 111. Quotations are made from this translation.

4. Seemingly the daily *Dreptatea* of the National Peasant Party. See footnote no. 12, Chapter III.

5. September 6, 1940 to August 23, 1944 when Marshal Ion Antonescu was head of State.

6. Two and half pages out of 7 1/2 of Rădescu's speech deal with "the agrarian problem".

7. For the English version of the second broadcast, see telegram no. 111 of the State Dept. (see footnote no. 1) and the Bucharest daily *Ultima Oră* of February 14, 1945.

8. *România Liberă*, III, no. 166, Wednesday, February 14, 1945, p. 3 and 4. Ilie Lazăr and Sergiu Fărcăşanu were known leaders of the National Peasant Party and of the National Liberal Party. Horaţiu Comaniciu was leader of the disbanded extreme right wing movement of the Iron-Guard. As many former members of the movement he had joined the NPP or the NLP, whilst others went to the communists or their affiliated groups.

9. *Ibidem*.

10. See note 8. The first comment of the same *România Liberă* no. 165 of Tuesday February 13, 1945, p. 3 was much more circumspect. The second day of the pro-communist press launched its all out war against the Prime Minister.

11. *România Liberă*, III, no. 167, Thursday, February 15, 1945, pp. 1–2; cablegram M 420 of February 14, 1945 from Bucharest; also Brigadier General C.V.R. Schuyler, US Army chief military representative to Major General J.E. Hull assistant Chief of Staff, OPD Pentagon Building – report from Bucharest, March 25, 1945, *Political developments in Romania*, pt. 4, the War Dept., National Archives, Washington, DC.

12. *R.L.*, III, no. 167, February 15, 1945, p. 2.

13. *Ibidem.*

14. *Idem*, p. 3.

15. "An important statement by NDF Council" in *România Liberă*, III, no. 162, Thursday February 8, 1945, p. 1. "If there is hunger in the country, minister Hudiţă is accountable for" said a comment published next day – *România Liberă*, no. 162, Friday February 9, 1945, p. 3; see also *România Liberă*, no. 164, Sunday February 11, 1945, p. 5.

16. *România Liberă*, III, no. 165, Monday February 12, 1945, p. 3.

17. "What happens at the Ministry of the Economy" by Alex. Corbu, *România Liberă*, III, no. 163, Saturday, February 10, 1945, p. 3.

18. See also *România Liberă*, III, no. 168 Friday February 16, 1945, p. 3.

19. Telegram no. 125 of February 19, 1945: 871.00B/2–1945, CS/EG State Dept., National Archives, Washington, DC.

20. Editorial by Nicolae Moraru, in *România Liberă*, III, no. 168, Friday February 16, 1945, p. 1 and 3.

21. Telegram no. 125 of February 19, 1945 (see footnote no. 19).

22. Telegram no. 124, of February 19, 1945: 871:00/2–1945 CS/EG, to the State Department. In February 1945, several thousands hectares

were forcibly seized by NDF activists and distributed to families of poor peasants in the county of Constanţa. See *România Liberă*, III, no. 173, p. 3.

23. Rădescu was actually the head of the interior department.

24. *Monitorul Oficial* (MO), vol CXIII, Part I, No. 41, Tuesday February 20, 1945, p. 1204; Decree Law no. 493 of February 19, 1945 and Burton Berry, US representative in Romania, to the State Department, Report no. 152 of March 13, 1945: 871.00/3–1345 CS, State Department, National Archives, Washington, DC, p. 2. Telegram of Teohari Georgescu to the prefects in *România Liberă*, III, no. 175, February 24, 1945, p. 3. Prefect = county chief representing the government.

Chapter V: The Incidents at the Malaxa Factory

1. *România Liberă*, Special Edition, III, no. 172, Wednesday February 21, 1945.

2. A two full pages report in *România Liberă*, III, no. 173, Thursday February 22, 1945, p. 1 and 3.

3. *Idem*, p. 1.

4. The Manifesto in *Scânteia* of February 22, 1945; "legionaries" i.e. members of the disbanded Iron Guard.

5. The Malaxa factory was producing mainly for the battlefront at that time.

6. There are no details when and how workers were arbitrarily detained. The whole account in *Dreptatea*, S. 2, no. 135, February 22, 1945.

7. *Ibidem*, and no. 138, Sunday February 25, 1945, p. 2.

8. Report dated March 25, 1945 by General Brigadier C.V.R. Schuyler to Major General J.E. Hull assistant Chief of Staff. The assessment on the Malaxa plant incidents in the chapter *Political Developments in Romania* pt. 5; similar account to the events by US representative in

Romania Burton Y. Berry to the State Department, on March 13, 1945: 871.00/3–1345, p. 1–2, National Archives, Washington, DC.

9. US Representation, Allied Control Commission for Romania, Bucharest, to the Allied Force Headquarters, Caserta, Italy, on March 16, 1945: War Dept., National Archives, Washington, DC.

Chapter VI: A Special Partner to the Communist Takeover: The Soviets. Preparations to the Last Drive to Power

1. *Scânteia*, II, no. 147, February 22, 1945, p. 1.

2. English translation of the handbills are annexed to report No. 152 by Burton Y. Berry US representative in Romania to the Secretary of State Department in Washington DC, on March 13, 1945: 871.00/3–1345, CS, State Department, National Archives, Washington, DC. See *Annexes*.

3. *Scânteia*, II, no. 149, February 24, 1945, p. 5. For English translation, see footnote no. 2. The handbill addressed to the army and distributed in Bucharest on February 23, 1945, included *Long Live the King, the Head of the Army*. This was possibly added to reassure the officers' corp which was almost totally devoted to the monarchy.

4. Same issue of *Scânteia*.

5. See for example the telegram of the Social Democratic Party to Marshal Stalin on the 27th anniversary of the Red Army, *Libertatea*, II, no. 162, Sunday February 25, 1945, p. 1.

6. Ploughmen's Front Appeal to the citizens, February 24, 1945.

7. *Scânteia*, III, no. 149, February 24, 1945, p. 1.

8. *România Liberă*, III, no. 176, February 25, 1945, pp. 1 and 3.

9. *Ibidem*.

10. An English translation of the *Pravda* article was sent by the US Mission at Bucharest to the State Department on February 23, 1945, as an annex to report no. 152 of March 13, 1945 (see footnote no. 2).

11. *Grai Nou*, II, no. 23 (63), Friday February 23, 1945, p. 1.

12. Both handbills annexed to US report no. 152 of March 13, 1945 (see footnote no. 2).

13. *The attitude of Mr. Maniu during the recent political crisis*, a confidential report by Burton Y. Berry, US representative in Bucharest, to the Secretary of State in Washington, dated March 1945, no. 161.

14. The first Sănătescu Government (August 23 – November 3, 1944) had the political backing of all four parties: the NPP, the Liberals, the Social Democrats and the Communists, all but the communist represented by their presidents.

15. The Appeal dated February 23, 1945 was published by *România Liberă*, III, no. 176, February 25, 1945, p. 1 and 5.

Chapter VII: Saturday, February 24, 1945

1. The categories are listed according to their significance for the Communist Party: workers first ...

2. *Scânteia*, II, no. 150, Sunday February 24, 1945, p. 1.

3. *România Liberă*, III no. 177, Monday February 26, 1945, p. 1.

4. Report no. 152 of March 13, 1945, p. 5 (see Chapter VI, footnote no. 2) and US military representative in Bucharest to the assistant Chief of Staff, report dated March 25, 1945, Chapter *Political Situation* ... pt. 5 (see Chapter V, footnote no. 8).

5. *Scânteia*, II, no. 151, Monday February 26, 1945, p. 4.

6. Some 350 yards from the Royal Palace Square.

7. The communist leaders Lucreţiu Pătrăşcanu, Constantin Doncea, Gheorghe Gheorghiu Dej, also Pătraşcu from the NDF and the social democrat Lothar Rădăceanu.

8. Military Examining Prosecutor Lieutenant Florin Olteanu wrote an official report on the events. The statement is dated February 24, 1945, 22:30 hours, and was written "in the building of the Ministry of Interior". It will be further referred to as: *Olteanu's report*. It is the most detailed report on the sequence of events. For the main developments Olteanu's report is confirmed by two US accounts on the same events (of March 13 and March 25) and by a synthesis of the demonstration to the general staff of the Military Command of Bucharest. See *Annexes*.

9. *Olteanu's report*, pt. 2 and 3.

10. A two pages report by Lieutenant-Colonel Magistrate Oreste Dobrotescu Military Examining Prosecutor, was completed during the night of February 25, 1945 after 1:00 a.m. It will be further referred to as *Dobrotescu's report*.

11. *Dobrotescu's Report*, p. 2.

12. *Olteanu's Report*, pt. 3.

13. *Ibidem*.

14. A Report on the demonstration of February 24, 1945 was submitted by Colonel Rădulescu, Commander of the Special Battalion of Gendarmes and by Lieutenant Magistrate Florin Olteanu to the General Staff of the Military Command of Bucharest. It states that the shots were fired from the Ilfov, Boteanu, Generala and Wilson apartment buildings. It will be further referred to as *Report to the general staff*.

15. *Olteanu's Report*, pt. 5.

16. *Olteanu's Report*, pt. 6.

17. *Ibidem*.

18. *Idem*, pt. 7.

19. *Report to the General Staff.*

20. *Ibidem*, also *Olteanu's Report*, pt. 8. The event is also in *Dobrotescu's Report*, pt. b.

21. *România Liberă*, III, no. 177, Monday February 26, 1945, p. 2.

22. Two nominal lists with the victims of the 24 February shootings are annexed to US representative's report no. 152 of March 13, 1945. The notes are certified by General I. Teodorescu, Military Commander of Bucharest.

23. The Soviet order is included in report no. 152 of March 13, 1945.

24. The Romanian acronym, of the National Democratic front was FND. It is also the acronym of "Fără Neam și Dumnezeu" which means in Romanian "The Nationless and Godless".

25. General Rădescu's broadcast on February 24, 1945 at 10:30 p.m. was not printed by the Romanian press under strict Soviet censorship at that time. An English translation is annexed to the US report no. 152 of March 13, 1945 (see Chapter VI, footnote no.2).

26. *Dobrotescu's Report*, pt. c.

27. Telegram M. 488 of February 28, 1945 from US representation, ACC Romania to the Allied Force Headquarters, Caserta, Italy: the War Dept., National Archives, Washington, DC.

28. An English translation annexed to the same US report no. 152 (see Chapter VI, footnote no. 2). The NLP expressed also its entire support for planned social reforms in favor of the workers and peasants and to fulfil all armistice obligations.

29. Report no. 152 of March 13, 1945, p. 8. The report added (page 5): "it seems clear that the shootings began from the edges of the crowd, from the demonstrators themselves, and a Russian patrol took up the challenge and fired, wounding many. The type of wounds which were made by pistols of non-Romanian army caliber apparently confirm this".

Chapter VIII: In The Wake Of The February 24 Events

1. *România Liberă*, III, no. 177, Monday February 26, 1945, p. 1 and 2.

2. *Idem*, p. 3 reproduced an alleged phone talk between an unidentified officer and an unidentified general from an unknown location. The officer allegedly called from the Royal Palace and said that the guard from the palace was firing upon the demonstrators. The phone call is told to have been mistakenly intercepted by a *România Liberă* staff who feigned to be the addressee of the phone call. This incident was never confirmed by any independent source. The names of those who made and received the phone call were never found out.
   There was a follow up in *România Liberă*, III, no. 180, Thursday March 1, 1945, p. 3.
   The Ministry of War Production issued a communiqué stating that four officers were present in the building of the ministry (not at the Royal Palace as the *România Liberă* version has suggested). One of the officers called general Diaconescu and dialled by mistake 53733 at the editorial board of *România Liberă* instead of dialing 53632. The officer had said over the phone that "fire arm shots were heard in the Royal Palace area". *România Liberă* rejected the communiqué of the War Production Ministry and alleged again that the officer said that the palace guard was firing. For the NDF version of events it was a paramount importance to portray the government as the one which staged the provocation. The communist comments in *România Liberă*, III, no. 180, Thursday March 1, 1945, p. 3.

3. *Scânteia*, II, no. 151, Monday February 26, 1945, p. 1.

4. *Ibidem*.

5. *România Liberă*, III, no. 177, Monday February 26, 1945, p. 1.

6. *Libertatea* of Tuesday February 27, 1945.

7. *România Liberă*, III, no. 180, Thursday March 1, 1945, p. 3. Negel's communiqué in US report no. 152. See *Annexes*.

8. *Scânteia* of Tuesday February 27, 1945.

9. *România Liberă*, III, no. 177, Monday February 26, 1945, p. 2.

10. *Scânteia*, II, no. 151, Monday February 26, 1945.

11. *România Liberă*, III, no. 177, Monday February 26, 1945, p. 1.

12. *Ibidem.* The nine ministers and deputy ministers were: Petre Groza, Gh. Gheorghiu Dej, Lothar Rădăceanu, Lucrețiu Pătrășcanu, Ștefan Voitec, G. Vlădescu Răcoasa, engineer Nicolau, Teohari Georgescu, Romulus Zăroni.

13. US report no. 152 of March 13, 1945, p. 8 (see Chapter VI, footnote no. 2).

14. *Scânteia*, II, no. 153, Thursday March 1, 1945, p. 1.

15. Telegram M 488 of February 28, 1945 from US Representation in Bucharest to AFH, Caserta, Italy, p. 4: War Dept., War Archives, National Archives, Washington, DC.

16. An English translation of the letter is annexed to Report no. 158 of March 15, 1945 from the US Mission in Bucharest, Romania to the Secretary of State: 871.00/3–1545. All quotations are from the four typed pages letter. See *Annexes*.

17. According to the resolution the members of the two parties ought to collaborate as closely as possible in all questions of political and trade union interests.

18. *România Liberă*, III, no. 180, Thursday March 1, 1945, p. 3. The eight members were: Dr. C.D. Parhon, Mihail Sadoveanu, Mitiță Constantinescu, Traian Săvulescu, Dr. D. Mezincescu, S. Stoilov, Dr. N.Gh. Lupu, prof. Dr. Hortolomei. Some, such as Parhon, Sadoveanu, Săvulescu and Mezincescu will be given political assignments in the late forties to fifties or sixties. All will be members of the new Academy nominated by the communist regime in 1948.

19. *Scânteia*, II, no.155 , of Friday March 2, 1945, p. 1. The letter is dated February 28, 1945.

20. *România Liberă*, III, no. 177 Monday February 26, 1945, front page. Same assertions in *Scânteia*, *Libertatea* (Social Democrat daily), *Frontul Plugarilor* (Dr. Petru Groza daily) etc.

21. *România Liberă*, III, no. 180, Thursday March 1, 1945, p. 1.

22. *România Liberă*, III, no. 177, Monday February 26, 1945, p. 2 and US Report no. 152, p. 5.

23. *R.L.*, III, no. 177, Monday February 26, 1945, p. 3.

24. *Ibidem.*

25. *Ibidem.*

26. With Marshal Antonescu's tacit consent, prince Barbu Ştirbey went to Cairo to start talks for Romania's surrender (March 1944).

27. Telegram no. 143 of February 28, 1945, US Mission in Bucharest to the Secretary of State: 871.00/2–2845. Prince Ştirbey had lunch with US representative Burton Berry on February 27.

28. *România Liberă*, III, no. 180, Thursday March 1, 1945, p. 1, headlined in one inch letters: "Radio Moscow has broadcast – the Rădescu Government must go".
The US Mission in Bucharest cabled to the War Department on February 28: "Meanwhile the Soviet press in Moscow has printed entirely erroneous account of the disorders charging that the fascist controlled Romanian government fired deliberately upon workers engaged in a peaceful demonstration": telegram M 488, p. 4, the War Department, National Archives, Washington, DC.

29. *Grai Nou*, II, no. 25 (65), Thursday March 1, 1945, p. 1 and no. 26 (66), Saturday March 3, 1945, p. 1 (editorials).

30. Telegram no. 606 of March 2, 1945, from Harriman US Ambassador at Moscow to the Secretary of State, Washington DC: 871.00/3–245, CS, National Archives, Washington, DC.

31. Report no. 158 of March 15, 1945 sent by Burton Y. Berry US representative in Romania, to the Secretary of State Washington DC, pp. 5–6: 871.00/3–1545, National Archives, Washington, DC.

Chapter IX: The Allied (Soviet) Control Commission On The Romanian Situation

1. *Resumé of the Conference of 14 February between Admiral Bogdenko, Mr. Pavlov and General Schuyler.* All quotations are from this document. It will be referred to as: *Resume: 871.00/3–845*, pp. 1–2.

2. *Idem*, p. 3.

3. *Idem*, p. 4.

4. Telegram M 425 of February 1945 from general Schuyler to Allied Force Headquarters, Caserta, Italy, p. 4: War Department, National Archives, Washington, DC. This telegram summarizes the discussions at the ACC on February 14, 1945.

5. The Transcript of the February 20 meeting was sent to the assistant Chief of Staff, the War Dept., on February 22 and to the State Dept., on March 8, 1945: 871.00/3–845, National Archives, Washington, DC. It will be referred to as *The transcript*.

6. The *Viitorul* daily of the National Liberal Party was suppressed on February 17 by ACC for "not very important reasons". *Dreptatea*, the National Peasants Party daily, wasn't printed by the workers union after February 12. *Curierul* an independent daily was suppressed on January 11, allegedly for not complying with censors regulations.

7. *The transcript*, p. 1–2.

8. *Idem*, p. 3.

9. *Idem*, pp. 3, 4.

10. The discussions over the incidents at Malaxa in *The transcript*, pp. 5, 6 and 7.

11. "If two Russian officers have gone there" said general Vinogradov, "they (i.e. Romanian government – D.C.G.) will realize that we are interested in the matter, and perhaps they will got some sense in their heads," *idem*, p. 6.

12. *Idem*, p. 7.

13. *Idem*, pp. 7–8.

14. *Idem*, p. 8.

15. *Idem*, pp. 10–11.

16. *Ibidem*.

17. *Idem*, pp. 10–11.

18. *Transcript and proceedings of the joint meeting of senior Russian, British and US representatives*, ACC Romania, 8:30 p.m., 21 February, 1945: 871.00/3–945, State Department, National Archives, Washington, DC. The transcript has 10 typed pages. The meeting was concluded at 9:15 p.m. (see page 10 of the *Transcript*).

19. *Scânteia*, II, No. 147, Thursday February 22, 1945, p. 1.

20. All quotations from the February 21, 1945 *Transcript* (see footnote no. 18).

21. "In order to insure the conditions under which the three governments will help the liberated nations to improve their economic and political conditions, a provisional government will be formed which will be composed of the representatives of all democratic elements until such time as a free election may be held. The three governments will consult each other on these questions, when in the opinion of the three governments the conditions in a particular country are such that the three governments find mutual consultations necessary, before taking the proper measure."

22. February 21, 1945, *Transcript*, pp. 5–6.

23. *Idem*, p. 9.

24. *Paper by the British commissioner for ACC* ..., annexed to *Resume* of ACC meeting on February 28, 1945: 871.00/3–2145, State Dept., National Archives, Washington, DC.

25. A copy of this statement was addressed to Lt. General Vinogradov. It was annexed to the *Transcript* dated February 21, 1945. Same content in the telegram no. M 483 from Schuyler, Bucharest to Allied Headquarters, Caserta, Italy, on February 28, 1945: War Dept., N.A.

26. Telegram M 444 of February 20, 1945 from General Schuyler to Allied Force Headquarters, Caserta, Italy, War Dept., N.A., p. 1. It will be referred to: *M 444*.

27. *Ibidem.*

28. *M 444*, p. 2, 3 and 4.

29. *M 444*, p. 4 and 5.

30. General Schuyler from Bucharest to Allied Headquarters, Telegram M 448 of February 20, 1945: p. 1, War Department, National Archives, Washington, DC.

31. *Idem*, p. 2.

32. Telegram M 467 of February 1945 from Schuyler to Allied Force Headquarters, Caserta, Italy: War Department, National Archives, Washington, DC.

33. Acting Secretary of State Grew to the War Dept., Washington DC. Telegram no. 86 of February 24, 1945.

Chapter X: The Dismantlement And Disarmament Of The Romanian Home Forces

1. The Armistice Convention article.

2. Alesandru Duţu, *Protocolul militar româno-sovietice din 26 octombrie 1944* (Romanian–Soviet Military Protocol of October 26, 1944), in *Revista Română de istorie militară*, no. 4, 1990, pp. 20–22 and 41. Marian Ştefan and Alesandru Duţu, *România în al doilea război mondial (V)* (Romania in World War II, part V) in *Magazin Istoric* October 1991, p. 37. General Gheorghe Mihail, Chief of the Romanian General Staff resigned in October 1944, unwilling to sign the Soviet imposed protocol.

3. *Resumé*, p. 4 (see Chapter IX, footnote no. 1).

4. For counselor Pavlov there had been no disagreements although gen. Gheorghe Mihail, the Romanian Chief of Staff resigned unwilling to sign the "convention". Thus the Soviet military authorities issued an ultimatum.

5. *Resumé*, p. 4 (see Chapter IX, footnote no. 1).

6. *Idem*, p. 4–5. A summarized version of the same informations is in Schuyler's Telegram M 425 of February 16, 1945, 4 pages: The War Dept., National Archives, Washington, DC.

7. Telegram no. 9413 of February 14, 1945 by General Schuyler to General Hull through Allied Force Headquarters, Caserta, Italy: War Dept., National Archives, Washington, DC. There are no checkings with the Romanian military archives of these figures till now.

8. See *The Transcript*, p. 13 (Chapter IX, footnote no. 5).

9. The report was forwarded to major general J.E. Hull, assistant Chief of Staff OPD, Pentagon Building. The report has four enclosures: Air section, Military situation, Political developments, Economic Developments: War Dept., National Archives, Washington, DC. The quotation is from the *Military situation*, p. 1.

10. *Ibidem*.

11. The Romanian Army was cited in seven orders of the day by the Supreme Soviet High Command. The gallantry of the Romanian troops was repeatedly cited by the Soviet communiqués: Gh. Romanescu, Nicolae Ciobanu, Alesandru Duţu, *L'Armee roumaine dans la campagne de l'ouest 1944–1945*, Editions militaires, Bucharest 1991, p. 259.

12. Telegram M 494 of March 2, 1945 from General Schuyler, Bucharest to Allied Force Headquarters, Caserta, Italy: War Department, National Archives, Washington, DC; also Schuyler's report to general J.E. Hull, p. 2 of *The military situation in Romania* (see footnote no. 9). According to Schuyler's report the ACC orders for additional reductions of the Romanian Home Army were issued on February 28 and became effective on March 1, 1945 (see *Air section* of the report).

13. See Schuyler's report to General J.E. Hull, *The Air Section* (see footnote no. 9).

14. The protest has been published by Lieutenant General (reserve) Ion Şuţa, *România la cumpăna istoriei* (Romania at History's Crossroads), Editura Ştiinţifică, Bucharest 1991, Annex no. 6, pp. 397–398.

15. See footnote no. 9: *The Military situation*, p. 1; and Telegram M 485 of February 28, 1945 and M 492 of March 1, from General Schuyler to Allied Force Headquarters, Caserta, Italy: War Dept., National Archives, Washington, DC.

16. Telegram M 485, p. 2 (see supra).

17. On March 3, 1945: *România Liberă*, III, no. 184, Monday March 5, 1945, p. 1.

18. Telegram M 492 of March 1, 1945 from General Schuyler to Allied Force Headquarters, Caserta, Italy (see footnote no. 15).

Chapter XI: Vishinsky Imposes a Communist Lead Government

1. The notes on A. Vyshinsky's audiences with King Mihai were taken by the Romanian interpreter Naum Ionescu on February 27–28, March 1 and 6, 1945. The notes are published in Romanian by Mircea Ciobanu, *Talks with Mihai I of Romania*, Humanitas Publishing House, Bucharest, 1991, pp. 238–244. The audience on February 27, 1945 at 9 p.m., at pp. 238–240.

2. *Idem*, pp. 240–241.

3. *Idem*, p. 241.

4. *Idem*, pp. 242–243.

5. According to the Romanian constitutions of 1866 and 1923 the King as the Chief of the State requested a Prime Minister to resign.

6. Telegram M 492 of March 1, 1945 from General Schuyler to AFH, Caserta, Italy, War Dept., Military Archives, National Archives, Washington, DC.

7. Telegram M 503 of March 1, 1945 from General Schuyler to AFH Caserta, Italy: War Department, Military Archives, National Archives, Washington, DC.

8. The statement is incorporated in the Report no. 158 of March 15, 1945 (see Chapter VIII, footnote no. 31).

9. *Grai Nou,* II, no. 20 (60), Saturday February 17, 1945, p. 1. (editorial)

10. Report no. 158, p. 6 (see footnote no. 8).

11. Telegram M 506 of March 6, 1945 from General Schuyler to AFH, Caserta, Italy: War Dept., Military Archives, National Archives, Washington, DC.

12. Telegram M 559 of March 16, 1945, *Ibidem.*

13. Telegram M 506 of March 6, 1945 (see footnote no. 11).

14. The National Peasant Party released a Communiqué with details on the events preceding the formation of the Groza Government. The Communiqué is annexed to report no. 158, as enclosure no. 5 and has two and half pages. It was not printed in the Romanian press. See *Annexes.*

15. The sequence of events is quoted from NPP Communiqué corroborated with other sources mentioned separately in each case.

16. See *România Liberă*, III, no. 186, Thursday March 8, 1945, p. 3.

17. The English version of both Communiqué is in the enclosure no. 4 to US Report no. 158. Telegram M 503 of March 3, pp. 2–3 (see footnote no. 7) says that the National Peasant Council, i.e. permanent delegation, met on March 3, 1945 at 10 a.m. and supported Maniu's position previously expressed to Groza in full (which meant the rejection of Groza's suggestion). US Report no. 158, p. 4 (see footnote no. 8) has the following comment on Groza's proposals to the NPP and NLP: "Dr. Petre Groza, for example, wished to name all

members of the National Peasant and National Liberal parties who would be included within his cabinet, whereas the party chiefs themselves when they finally agreed to cooperate in a Groza dominated cabinet, held out for naming their own men." See *Annexes*.

18. Telegram M 503, p. 2 (see footnote no. 7).

19. Namely: Ştefan Voitec (Education), Lothar Rădăceanu (Labor) and Tudor Ionescu (Mines and Petrol). The latter was nicknamed "the plastographer" since he presented a forged letter at the Social Democratic Congress of March 1946 to get the ousting of all independent Social-Democrat leaders. The dissident National Peasants were a tiny splinter group which sided with NDF after the February 24, 1945 events.

20. Namely: Teohari Georgescu (Interior), General Vasiliu Răşcanu (at that time still posing as professional officer), Petre Constantinescu-Iaşi (Informations), Lucreţiu Pătrăşcanu (Justice), and Gh. Gheorghiu Dej (Communications). Emil Bodnăraş considered one of the most hard liner communist leader of that time, was proposed as undersecretary for "order and security". The whole proposed governmental list is annexed to the US report no, 158, enclosure 2, see also Telegram M 503 of March 3, 1945. See *Annexes*.

21. The details from the NPP Communiqué. See footnote no. 14 and *Annexes*.

22. US Report no. 161 from Bucharest, March 17, 1945, to the Secretary of State: 871.00/3–1745 CS MAJ. N.A., p. 3.

23. *Ibidem*.

24. National Peasant Party Communiqué, p. 2.

25. US Report no. 158, p. 6 (see footnote no. 8).

26. See for example *România Liberă*, III, no. 186 of March 8, 1945, p. 2 and 4, with an extended coverage of the mass demonstration of March 6. The 50,000 one could add some 10–15,000 if all the incoming streets were packed with people.

27. *România Liberă*, III, no. 187, Friday March 9, 1945, p. 1 and 3.

28. *Ibidem.* See also US Mission Bucharest Report no. 158 of March 15, 1945, p. 7.

29. *Era Nouă* of March 12, 1945.

30. For the National Peasant Party Communiqué, see footnote no. 14.

31. *Ibidem.*

Chapter XII: Back to the Allied (Soviet) Control Commission on the Latest Developments

1. Resumé of proceedings of joint meeting of senior Russian, British and United States representatives, ACC Romania, 20:00 hours, 28 February 1945: 871.00/3–2145, State Dept., National Archives, Washington, DC. The resumé has two and one third typed pages and is signed by brigadier General C.V.R. Schuyler.

2. The British letter to A. Vyshinsky is annexed to the US Resumé. Same content in telegram M 489 of March 1, 1945 from General Schuyler to AFH, Caserta, Italy: War Dept., National Archives, Washington, DC.

3. Quoted from the *Resumé* pp. 1 and 3.

4. Telegram M 485 of February 28, 1945, from General Schuyler to the War Dept., National Archives, Washington, DC.

5. Resumé of the Conference between Colonel General Susaikov, Deputy Chairman of ACC and General Schuyler. The Resumé was sent from Bucharest on March 5, 1945. A copy was sent to the State Dept. on March 21, 1945: 871.00/3–2145, National Archives, Washington, DC.

6. All quotations at the March 4th meeting are from the *Resumé*.

7. Report of Brigadier General Schuyler to Major Colonel J.E. Hull assistant Chief of Staff, Pentagon Building, March 25, 1944, p. 1: War Dept., National Archives, Washington, DC.

8. See the Resumé, pt. 4 (footnote no. 5). A summary of the talks at this meeting in General Schuyler's Telegram M 509 of March 5, 1945: War Dept., National Archives, Washington, DC. The communist press in Romania used the same wording as General Susaikov.

9. Transcript of discussion at Conference between the Colonel General Susaikov and Brigadier General Schuyler 3:30 p.m., 5 March 1945: 871.00/3–2145. State Dept., National Archives, Washington, DC. The transcript has six typed pages and is signed by Brigadier General Schuyler; all the quotations are from the transcript.

10. *Idem*, p. 5.

11. *Resume...* of March 21, 1945 (footnote no. 5).

12. Telegram M 485 from General Schuyler to the War Department: on February 28, 1945; War Department Archives, National Archives, Washington, DC.

13. Telegram M 492. General Schuyler to AFH, Caserta, Italy: *ibidem*.

14. Telegram M 503 of March 3, 1945 from General Schuyler to AFH, Caserta, Italy, p. 2: *ibidem*.

Chapter XIII: Winston Churchill, Franklin Delano Roosevelt and Andrei Vishinsky on the February Events In Romania

1. Paraphrase of the Telegram sent by the Prime Minister to the President on March 8th, no. 905: 871.00/3–1045 CYC, State Department; almost the same text is incorporated in Winston Churchill's *The Second World War – Triumph and Tragedy*, Bantam Books, New York, 1962, pp. 361–361; also in FRUS, 1945, vol. V, pp. 505–506.

2. The draft of the answer was presented to President Roosevelt by Secretary of State E.R. Stettinius Jr. on March 10, 1945. It was "approved and sent ... without change" the next day: 871.00/3–1045. CJC, State Dept.; also in FRUS, 1945, vol. V, pp. 509–510.

3. *Ibidem*.

4. US ambassador Harriman from Moscow to the Secretary of State Washington DC. telegram no. 3227 of September 10, 1945: 871.00/3–1045 State Dept., pp 1–2, National Archives, Washington, DC.

5. Telegram no. 3251 on September 12, 1945: 871.00/3–2145, State Dept., p. 1, National Archives, Washington, DC.

6. Telegram M 523 of March 8, 1945 from General Schuyler to AFH, Caserta, Italy: War Dept., National Archives, Washington, DC.

7. *Ibidem.*

8. Report no. 161 of March 1945 by Burton Berry from Bucharest, to the State Dept., pp. 2–3: 871.00/3–1245 CS/MAJ, State Dept., National Archives, Washington, DC.

ANNEXES

Document no. 1

National Archives,
Washington D.C. 871.00/3-545

Embassy of the United States of America
Near the Polish Government

London, March 5, 1945

The Honorable
The Secretary of State,
Washington, D.C.

Sir:

I have the honor to enclose for the Department's information a copy of a report entitled *The Development of the Political Situation in Romania, December 1944 – January 1945* dated Istanbul, February 1, 1945, made available by the Chief of Polish Political Intelligence.

Respectfully yours,
Rudolf E. Schoenfeld,
Charge d'Affaires ad interim

Enclosure:
1/ report as stated.

SECRET

Enclosure No. 1 to Dispatch
Polish Serie 730, March 5, 1945
Istanbul, February 1st, 1944

The Development of the Political Situation in Romania (December 1944 – January 1945)

During the first days of December 1944, at the moment of the resignation of the second Sănătescu's Cabinet, both the democratic Romanian circles and the foreign observers seriously expected if not an open coup d'etat on the part of the Communists, then an attempt to a quasi legal taking over of the power by them by way of eliminating the Democratic representatives, viz. the Agrarians and the Liberals from the Government. The cover under which the Communists were expected to hide their dictatorship was the so-called National-Democratic organizations, such as *The Patriotic Union*, *The Peasant Front*, also that group of Socialists, who fully collaborate with them, as well as the Social-Popular Party of Ralea.

Already at the end of November in the Press and at the meetings of the National-Democratic Front threats were openly made that the power would be taken over by the "people", whereas the Government was accused of harbouring the Fascists, of not fulfilling of the armistice conditions, of withholding the introduction of social reforms, etc. These attacks were seconded by the Soviet broadcasts. Consequently it looked like as if the coup d'etat was a question of a few days. Furthermore the activities developed by Vice-Commissar Vishinsky, during his four weeks (November 7, 1944 – December 8, 1944) stay in Romania confirmed the public opinion in its expectations. Vishinsky's activities openly proceeded in the direction of instigating revolutionary tendencies and undermining the position of the bourgeois parties. He did not establish any real collaboration with the Romanian Government avoided conversations with Maniu and Brătianu, whilst, on the other hand, he spent his time in conferences with Communist leaders and those Democratic leaders who would be willing to be used as tools for the provocation of splits in their own parties.

When on December 2nd, the Cabinet crisis became obvious, it was generally supposed that the Communists will attempt to stage a coup d'etat. In order to elucidate finally the designs of the Communists and to make them responsible for the events, the Zaranists and the Liberals decided to leave the Coalition Government. King Michael then entrusted General Rădescu with the formation of the new Cabinet. In spite of a certain popularity which Rădescu has been enjoying in the leftist circles owing to his firm stand vis a vis the Germans during Antonescu's regime, the Communist Press hailed his nomination as a provocation, and demanded if the National-Democratic Front were to remain in the Government, besides the portfolios already in their possession, also the portfolios of the Interior and of National Defence. This demand could not be accepted, as it would mean that the Government were in the hands of the Communists, though the responsibility would also be shared by the Democratic Parties.

At the critical moment (December 4th) came the King Michael's intervention which was both skilful and successful. By the way, the King despite his young age has shown a certain political talent and consequently he enjoys great popularity in the entire country. Thus the King called Vishinsky and told him that the activities of the Communist Party if continued may lead the country to anarchy. The King does not feel to be strong enough to keep order and law, if the Soviets and their representatives in Romania continue to support or even tolerate the anarchic activities of the Communists. Consequently if the Soviet Government decides to patronize further Communist activities, he would have no proper conditions for the fulfilment of the constitutional role, and thus he would have to abdicate and leave the country. Furthermore the King stated that he told Rădescu not to endeavor any more to form a coalition Government but to try to form one composed of non-political specialists. Vishinsky, according to serious sources, was surprised both by the contents and the firm form of the King's pronouncement. He gave a noncommitting reply, but at the same time denied his responsibility for the activities of the Communists, quoting the well-known declaration of Molotov, dated April 2nd, 1944, regarding the non-interference into Romania's internal affairs, and finally said that Russia is only interested in a speedy and accurate fulfilment of the armistice terms by Romania.

On December 5th, General Rădescu told the Communists that the Democratic Parties rejected their ultimatum demanding the posts of Ministry of the Interior and the National Defence. Consequently he, on the King's orders, is forming a non-political Cabinet. In fact in the afternoon of the same day, thanks to Maniu's efforts behind the scene, the list of the new Cabinet was ready. The Ministers were to take oath on the same evening. In the meantime the Communists received instructions from Vishinsky to withdraw their demands, and thus they immediately informed Rădescu that they agree to the former form of a Coalition

Government. On the 6th December, the new Cabinet was sworn in. It differed from the old one by the change on the post of the Premier, who also took over the post of the Minister of the Interior formerly held by Penescu, who was hated by the Communists.

It would be too naive to say that the King's intervention alone was sufficient to make Vishinsky change his mind and to recall the Communists from the streets of Bucharest. But it was due to Vishinsky's decision on which the King's action had undoubtedly an influence. Vishinsky's mission could be compared with that which Zdanov had, at one time, to fulfil in the Baltic States: the preparation of a basis for Sovietization. Vishinsky's activities were thus experimental. At first he encouraged the Communists to more energetic activities and attempts to take over the power. At the same time he watched the reaction of the Democratic circles. Soon he came to the conclusion that despite the passivity of these circles and lack of will to resistance, the Romanian masses were in great majority hostile to Communism, and that the Communist Party was so weak, not only as regards quantity but also quality, that it would not be able to cope with the administration. If, in addition, the King were to abdicate, then the whole Soviet gamble would be discovered prematurely, and consequently the Russians would have to take the administration into their own hands. This would not be appropriate just at that moment because of Russia's policy towards the Anglo-Saxon countries. Consequently Vishinsky decided to slow down and thus he ordered a temporary pause, instead of a coup d'etat. How much Russia did not want to have at that moment any complications is best shown by the fact, that after the conversation with the King, Vishinsky decided to leave Romania immediately. He thus left, as he had come, without notice, on December 8th, though he had previously accepted invitations for later dates. A relaxation in the internal situation has been noticed at once. The Communist Press has changed its tone. Meetings and street manifestations have ceased. The attacks by the Soviet radio have also been stopped. Even Vishinsky, before his departure, publicly announced, thus denying the statements made by the Communist Press, that "the fulfilment of the armistice terms has made certain progress, though there still remains a lot to be done." Though the Communist papers have continued to carry on propaganda for the introduction of social reforms, nevertheless they gave up encouraging the workmen to take over factories and land estates, and some time later even the attacks on the bourgeois parties and their leaders have been suspended.

The penetration of Communism goes, of course, forward, but it is obvious that the Communists follow Vishinsky's instructions to apply, for the time being, purely tactical methods. They have simply slackened their tempo in order to gather strength, which they lacked for the decisive blow. First of all, they maintain the posts formerly gained. Thus administration of Moldavia remains entirely in their hands, as well as that of many larger cities (Constanța, Ploiești, Hunedoara, etc). The same applies to those factories and trade unions which they have been able to take over. As regards the administration of Moldavia, they even gained a new success, for the inter-ministerial commission had confirmed their men in office in the nine most important prefectures out of the total of sixteen. The other seven prefects are: 3 Liberals, 2 Zaranists and 2 non-Party men. The accepted principle that each Communist Prefect should have a Democratic Vice-prefect, had so far not been kept by the Communists.

They do not either keep the promise made to the Democratic Parties, when the coalition agreement was renewed at the formation of Rădescu Government. They then promised to disband the Communist militia and agreed to elections to the local governments. The militia counts some 10-12,000 members, and is mostly concentrated in the capital. It is composed of the worst elements, and though it does not represent any real force, it can always be used as an instrument to provoke disturbances, which would then justify the introduction of Soviet troops. The Communists continue also to oppose the elections to local government bodies, as they are afraid that the results could prove their weakness and the introduction of legally elected local government authorities, in place of those which they introduced by force under the pretext of "liquidating the Fascists". All the illusions as to the stability of the "truce" between the Communists, and the Democrats have however finally disappeared when the National-Democratic Front published its New Year's appeal to the Romanian People. This appeal constituted the breaking off the truce, in any case of that which existed in the Press. In long and chaotic phraseology it repeated all the charges against the Democratic Parties, and especially against the Zaranists. It became quite apparent that the present coalition with the Democrats, the Communists consider as a temporary arrangement. In a most brutal manner they attacked the Zaranist "Iuliu Maniu Guard", which acted in Transylvania immediately after the liberation, calling it "a band of terroristic-chauvinistic criminals." The appeal denies that the coalition administration has done anything in order to fulfil the terms of the armistice, and repeats the Communist demands, such as the carrying out of the agrarian reform within 6 weeks, a general purge beginning with the waiters of the clergy, etc.

Simultaneously within the Cabinet the Communists and their satellites have been continuing their methods of sabotaging all the work of the Government, trying to force through the laws which they favour, and to disorganize the life of the country in general. The main aim of the Communists has been lately to secure for themselves in a legal way the monopoly of organizing the trade unions, and to have the act regarding war criminals worded in such a way that it would allow them to liquidate anyone whom they considered to be hostile to their plans. After discussions lasting for some weeks, the Democratic wing of the Government succeeded however in defending partially those two problems. The decree regarding the trade unions is based on the principle of liberty of organization. This means that besides the unions already in existence and which are led by the Communists other unions may be organized. Thus the Zaranists plan to create their own network of unions. Nevertheless the preponderance of Communists in those organizations seems to be secured. Some of the unions have already been taken over by them. Amongst them are the unions of Journalists, Writers, Printers, and certain Unions of metal workers. In other unions they try to obtain the majority by means of terror in factories or by means of administrative pressure, as for instance, in the case of the railway workers, taking advantage of the fact that the Minister of Communication is an active Communist. As regards the act regarding War Criminals, it was possible to pass a more or less exact definition of the crimes, thus to a certain extend to avoid a free interpretation for political aims. In any case the Communist project of creation a People's Court, which would be free to give its own interpretation of the law fell through. The Communists carry on propaganda for the immediate execution of the agrarian reform, which should apply to all land property above 50 hectares. The Democratic Parties affirm that the agrarian reform executed after the First World War was radical, and in practice the amount of land available for distribution is exceedingly small, if the model, experimental or industrial estates are to be exempted. The communists, however, compile fantastic statistics proving that 32% of the land, which means 5 million ha., is available for distribution, whereas the economists of the Democratic Parties affirm that the estates possessing over 50 ha. form only 750,000 to 1.4 million ha.

The Liberals and the Zaranists are unable to counteract strongly enough the constant pressure of the Communists. Their participation in the King's intervention of December 4th, was also secondary. Their success in the matter of the two law acts was possible because the Communists retreated not wanting to split the coalition prematurely. The internal weakness of the Democrats has best been seen in the decision arrived at by the inter-ministerial commission for the settlement of administrative matters in Moldavia. Though the majority of the members of the Commission belong to the Liberal and Zaranist Parties, they not only agreed to confirm the prefects wilfully installed by the Communists, but on their return to Bucharest expressed their thanks to the communists for their will for collaboration, and avoid any mention of their acts of violence, put the whole blame for the chaos existing in Moldavia on the Antonescu administration.

The two Democratic Parties, and especially the Zaranists, which have been the backbone of the Romanian Democracy, are going through an acute internal crisis. Like in the majority of the European countries the Democratic groups in Romania suffer from the lack of prominent leaders. Maniu is still a symbol, but his age prohibits him for intensive activity. Thus, in view of many and complicated problems, which are cropping up daily, differences of opinion inside the Party are growing. The Peasant Party which is the result of an amalgamation of the Conservative Peasants from Transylvania with the more Radical group of so-called "Old Kingdom" (as before 1914) has never been an entirely unified political organization. Today those differences are still more coming to the surface. Thus owing to conflicts of personal character between these two groups the Zaranists lost the post of Minister of Interior in the Rădescu Cabinet, as they could not agree to one candidate. In the matter of agrarian reform their views are also not united. The Transylvanians are more conservative, whereas the "Royalists" would not mind agreeing to small concessions to the Communists. To this is to be added the action, though of little importance, but which increases the chaos, of Dr. Lupu, who has been chosen by the Communists and approved by Vishinsky, as the man who is to split the Peasant Party from within.

The Liberals are still involved in the conflict dating from 1934: the conflict between the "old" Liberals headed by Dinu Brătianu, and the "young" ones under Tătărescu. The latter, whilst Maniu and Brătianu refused to collaborate with him because of his servility to Carol II, has found more understanding with the Russians. When the Democratic newspapers one after another are being liquidated because of "lack of paper" Tătărescu has obtained a fair amount of newsprint from the Russians and started the publication of a paper *Drapelul*; he is also organizing a political party on his own.

The Communist Party also lives through an internal crisis. This however is not shown externally, and when the difficulties are getting more acute, then they are settled in an authoritative manner by an order from Moscow. At this very moment there exists a conflict between Moscow envoys, Anna Pauker and Luca Laszlo, on one hand, and Minister Pătrăşcanu, on the other. The role of the present General Secretary Pârvulescu is also not quite clear. But all these conflicts are well kept inside the organization, and in their external moves the Communists remain united.

Besides the internal difficulties the greatest concern of the Romanian Government is the matter of its relations with the Soviet Government. In this matter the December "relaxation" has perhaps been most apparent. Though during the last weeks the Kremlin has addressed new and serious demands, nevertheless the Soviet Government's tendency is to appear lenient in its policy vis a vis Romania, in any case for the time being. The motives are the same as those which made Vishinsky to issue instructions to the Communists to be more moderate in their action. Thus during December, the Soviet Authorities were showing more confidence to the Rădescu Government, and also more understanding in certain matters. This did not however mean that in other matters, which the Kremlin considered to be of great importance, the Russians didn't act with extreme ruthlessness.

A heavy blow to the prestige of the Rădescu Administration was the confiscation by General Vinogradov of the Premier's two declarations intended for the Press. On December 30th, the Premier made an official statement to the Press and foreign correspondents regarding the policy of the Government. The aim of the Premier was to appeal to the Soviets and Allies to ease their policy towards Romania by not burdening her with too heavy economic demands. Though this appeal was worded very cautiously, General Vinogradov confiscated the two declarations, notwithstanding the fact that the contents of one of them had already been made known to a large number of journalists and had also been broadcast. General Rădescu strongly protested and even threatened to resign but General Vinogradov refused to alter his decision.

The most serious impression has however been made on the Romanian public opinion by the deportation to Russia of Romanian citizens of German origin and of Romanians originating from Bessarabia and Northern Bukovina who took refuge in Romania proper before the Russian advance and whom Russians claim to be Russian citizens. This Russian step has shown the entire illusiveness of Romania's independence. The deportation of Romanian citizens of German origin constitutes a serious precedent, as it is being applied not only to people who actively collaborated with the Nazis, but to all men of ages between 17 and 45 and women between 18 to 30. The interpretation of who is a German is very vague, sometimes it is enough to have one parent of German blood, or just a German sounding surname. Thus people belonging to families which had been "Romanized" for two or three generations, are being deported and many of them very often do not even speak the German language. Out of the entire number of 590,000 Romanians of German origin, some 300,000 threatened with deportation. The Soviet authorities are carrying on arrests and the deportation without any reference to the Romanian authorities. The deportees are being taken away in unheated trucks and sometimes even in open lorries. Officially it is being said that labour units will be formed of these deportees. If only people who had been collaborating with the Nazis, were deported probably no objections would have been raised, but in fact persons who have nothing in common with the Germans or political activities are suffering. Another aspect of this matter is that the Soviet authorities without the knowledge and consent of the Romanian authorities are taking away citizens of a country with which they signed an armistice. Thus Romanian public opinion is justly concerned that the same treatment might be soon applied to all the Romanians, who would oppose the Sovietization of Romania. The protest lodged by the Rădescu Government met with no success, and only after an energetic protest on the part of the Americans, the Soviets agreed to form mixed Russo-Romanian Commission which is to select the deportees. The reaction of the country was so strong that the Liberals were prepared to leave the Cabinet, but the Zaranists persuaded them to change their decision so as not to give the Communists the opportunity to say that the Democrats are taking the Germans under their protection. Finally the matter has been dealt with by Marshal Malinowski, who came to Bucharest at the beginning of January. It was been decided that only those Romanians who signed the German Volksliste will be due for deportation. It is not, however, certain that the decision will be final, as rumors say that the Kremlin still insists on the realization of the deportation according to their first instructions. It is also said that certain misunderstandings have arisen in connection with this matter between the central Russian authorities and General Vinogradov, who might be sent to Helsinki to take over a similar post there.

The deportation to Russia of refugees from Bessarabia and Northern Bukovina and which the Russians claim to be an act of repatriation has also caused many comments. The number of people involved in this amounts to some 12,000. As Soviet citizens the Russians consider even persons who lived there during the period from July 1940 to June 1941. A great majority of those people does not want to go back, being well aware that it does not mean repatriation but deportation to Russia. Only a few small group had applied for a return on its own free will.

Another instance of pressure on the part of the Soviets is the demand to reduce the Romanian Army to three divisions, excepting the fourteen divisions fighting in Hungary, and the reduction of the Police and Military Police to half of its present strength.

In the field of economy the Russians make constantly new demands. In January they demanded the handing over the machinery from many electrical power stations, 20% of machinery of the textile industry and a certain proportion of machinery of the metal industry. From Moldavia to Transylvania the Russian troops have already been taking away factory plants for some time past. The loss of textile machinery is just now of less importance, as owing to lack of raw material the production has had to be greatly curtailed. What is worse is that the value of those plants is not being charged to the reparation account, but it is to be considered as a payment on account of money due for the upkeep of Russian troops of occupation. The loss of the electrical plant and metal industry machinery is a very severe blow to Romanian economy, as they cannot be soon replaced and they had always been scarce.

In general in the field of economy it is obvious that though the Soviets are trying to exploit Romania to the utmost, they want to avoid a final economic catastrophe. Thus for instance after four months of totally free exploitation of the country's supplies, General Malinowski signed in January some kind of a commercial agreement, by which a system has been established regarding the manner of debiting the goods supplies to the 300 million reparation account. Another concession applies to a more free use of the railways for the needs of the country.

In general the economic situation is getting worse from week to week. It will not be an exaggeration to say that the country is threatened with hunger and ruin. This was emphasized by General Rădescu in his dramatic appeal of December 30th, and since that time the situation has been becoming even more desperate. The prices have been going up constantly. The reasons are political difficulties, as well as economic and transport difficulties. The railways are almost entirely engaged in carrying Soviet military transport, this coupled with the insecurity of road transport, deprives the cities of supplies, and causes the prices of commodities to rise. The cost of living has thus gone up as follows: 1939 – 100; 1st September 1944 – 1300; 25th December 1944 – 2800. Fuel and lubricates 1st September 1944 -1050, 25th December 1944 – 3200. The dearth has forced the Government to raise the salaries and pays. The budget is in a state of chaos. Nevertheless the Government gained a certain success for the internal loan offered at the beginning of January was satisfactory subscribed. It is being said that the gold will be released in order to support the value of the Leu.

The main aim of the Romanian Trade Delegation which arrived in Ankara for negotiations has been to secure supplies of Turkish coal. The Romanian coal mines at Petroşani produce minimal amounts of coal. Also a lack of being felt of petrol which was used not only on Romanian railways but also for heating purposes in private homes. Romanians hope re-establish maritime communication with Turkey within the next two months.

In the sphere of cultural life Soviet propaganda is extremely active. In all towns, even in the smallest, and in the villages branches of the Romanian Society for Cultural Cooperation with the USSR have been opened. This Society has at his disposal large sums of money and many facilities such as films, lending libraries, etc.

The Romanian Democrats have no more illusion as to the final aims of the Soviet policy. For some time past the hopes of the Romanians were directed towards the Anglo-Saxon countries, and consequently their reserved attitude has become for the Romanian Democrats a matter of deep disillusionment, though nothing else could have been expected. Realizing this the Romanians accepted the tactic of wait and see. They wish to continue the rather artificial coalition policy which still hampers the activities of the Communists. They would like to endure this state of affairs until the Germany is beaten, still thinking that perhaps then Anglo-Saxons not being so much dependent on Russia's help, might adopt a more active policy in the Balkans. The recent statement made in the British Parliament regarding Romania's effort in the fight against Germany has been received by the Romanian public opinion with great satisfaction. On the other hand, however, the hopes for Anglo-Saxon help are steadily fading out, all the more when it is realized that the Inter-Allied Commission exists only in name, whilst Romania is being ruled by General Vinogradov, the chief of the Soviet delegation of this Commission. The Anglo-Saxon delegations do not even participate in the meetings of the Commission, and the decisions passed by the Soviet delegates are sent for their information ex-post. The Romanians are already aware that the Anglo-Saxon delegates are only observers, and the decisions in almost all matters are taken by Moscow, sometimes with the knowledge and consent of London and Washington.

As regards the foreign policy of Romania, it concerns only one matter, viz. the Hungarian problem. This problem has not yet finally been decided by the Allies, and thus Romania's endeavors may bring some success. The formation of the Hungarian Government at Debreczen and the signing of the armistice provoked great interest in Romania. Great satisfaction has been expressed that the Hungary has undertaken to return Romania Northern Transylvania. The Miklosz Government has been accepted with the feeling of relief, for it was feared that the new Government might be composed entirely of Communists or of crypto-Communists. A tendency, though still a very slight one, has been noticed to seek an understanding with Hungary. The leaders of the Democratic groups, and especially of the Zaranist Party, committed a serious mistake by keeping up in the masses a hatred towards the Hungarians, though it was obvious that the fate of Transylvania will be decided by the Great Powers and not by the feelings of the population. Instead of looking for contacts with Hungary on the basis of common dangers and difficulties due to the two countries' relations, first with the Germans and then with the Russians, the Zaranists maintained their anti-Hungarian attitude even when Transylvania has officially been allotted to Romania. This attitude has perfectly suited the political designs of the Communists and the Soviets, for in present situation Russia becomes the protector not only of the Hungarian minority in Romania, but also of Hungary itself, vis a vis

Romania, which will come out of the war much stronger than Hungary. Only now the Romanians begin to realize that the so-called Hungarian danger was in reality a fake, supported by the policy of the Great Powers, at first by Germany and later by the Russians. Though many Romanians realize this now, it is still difficult to foresee whether the two countries will find a common language of understanding.

Document no. 2

National Archives, Washington D.C.,
Press General No. 165/1945
United States Mission
Bucharest, Romania

General Rădescu's Speech
February 11th 1945

Ladies and Gentlemen!

I am deeply moved.

I cannot find words to thank you for the enthusiastic reception you have accorded me, except by assuring you that, as I have done my duty the two months I have been at the head of the Government, so will I do it to the end.

The appeal I made to the population of the Capital gave rise to many objections. It was even suggested to me that I should give up the idea. I refused. I thought fit to maintain my point of view, for the following two reasons:

In the first place, I am not a party man. The groups in my Government belonging to different parties have each their own press and the opportunity of holding meetings, where they can have their say. But I, who cannot take part in meetings, can never say what I think.

On the other hand, as a confirmed democrat, I consider that I could find no better way of showing the democratic spirit with which I am deeply imbued, than by coming before you from time to time to keep you informed of the situation of the country, and to ask for opinion of my activity; whether you are satisfied or dissatisfied, you will show your approval or disapproval.

This is the reason of my presence here before you; to get into touch with you and discuss the problems I propose to submit to you all, for your approval or disapproval.

I have of course no intention of carrying on polemics with anyone. However, I reserve the right to say what I think, the same right as is enjoying by every subject of the country.

Ladies and Gentlemen!

From the moment His majesty the King (*cheers!*) graciously entrusted me with the Government of the country, I declared firmly that the basic points of the policy which the government I headed intended to pursue were the following:

1. The prosecution of the war to the utmost beside the Allies, until the final defeat of Hitlerism (*prolonged cheers!*).

2. The loyal and unhesitating fulfilment of the conditions of the armistice concluded with the allies (cheers).

3. The maintenance of order, so that we may all work calmly yet intensely to increase production, and thus meet the engagements which we have contracted by the armistice terms (*cheers*).

For the realization of these objects, I have fought indefatigably, without sparing myself, without rest (*cheers*).

Taking into account the very serious situation through which we are passing, I may state that the results obtained may be considered satisfactory. There are of course certain reservations to be made, but, I repeat, in the exceptionally difficult conditions of today, I do not think that more could be demanded of us.

If, however, there are still carping critics who constantly try to discredit the superhuman efforts which are being made to make things run as smoothly as possible, and who at each step level accusations at those who are burdened with the conduct of affairs, it is not incomprehensible. Political passions have always been rife in our country, and it is not different now. And, as has always been the case, there are ungovernable ambitions, and those who are filled with them can find no rest. They struggle continuously, and try, even at the price of the country's subjection, to satisfy their desires. (shouts of: *That is so!*).

And then there are people whom a state of chaos suits, since in a state of chaos anyone can find the opportunity to plot. (cries of: *Shame!*)

In considering things today, I have no intention of allowing myself to be side-tracked into polemics, because that is not my object today. To establish the truth, however, I must reveal things to the country, in their true light. (*cheers*)

No one can deny that things are not going quite as everyone would like, that there are not shortcomings, that mistakes are not made. I am the first to admit this. I completely disagree however with those who make it their creed to see only bad in all that is being done, and who bring all kinds of absurd charges and wittingly insinuate that it is all bad faith, ill will and sabotage, and that all those in places or responsibility are Nazis, Fascists, Hitlerists and all kind of monsters; words which have become so banal, so ridiculous, that everyone laughs, if he is not indignant, at the sound of them. And it would be no great loss if only smiles were the result of these base insinuations. Unfortunately, they cause deep seated harm, which, if those concerned realize them, should make them trouble.

In coping with the demands entailed by the armistice, we sometimes come up against unimaginable difficulties due to complete lack of means in some departments, which sometimes gives rise to shortcomings in execution; since the fishers in troubled waters can hardly wait for a chance to throw the blame for everything on the Hitlerism, sabotage, etc., are the Allies not right in thinking that it is really bad faith, when in fact it is only lack of means? (*cheers*)

There may however be some insignificant good-for-nothings who try to complicate matters, but to calling Ministers reactionary saboteurs is going too far.

As I have said, such a poisonous campaign conducted so implacably is not without meaning. In the politics of Romania, slander has always had a leading place. But if at other times, the slandering of one political party by another could only hit those it was intended to hit, now it has its repercussions on the entire country, and its consequences may be incalculable.

I believe therefore that I am right to demand that this harmful system of political conflict should cease. I also feel justified in protesting against the charges brought against my collaborators. The epithet of saboteur or reactionary may not be thrown at any Minister. I insist on that, since it would be painful and harmful if our Allies harboured any doubts as to he good intentions of the members of the government.

Can anyone believe that I, who have made the rigorous fulfilment of the Armistice conditions a point of honour, and the principal aim of whose policy has been the closest possible relations with the Soviet Russia, should allow myself to stand beside colleagues at whom such grave accusations are levelled? As an end must be put to such state of things, I think it necessary to clear away other accusations which are made against some members of the Government.

I am referring to the question of war-criminals and of those responsible for the country's disaster.

I personally have done my utmost that this thorny problem should be settled as early as possible. To this end an inter-ministerial commission was set up, composed of delegates of all groups in the country, presided over by the Vice-President of the Council of Ministers, which was to draw up the list of the accused. The lists were brought up for discussion before the Council of Ministers, where they were unanimously approved. (*cheers*) This was the way in which the work was carried out. If there is any blame to be cast, can it be cast on one or the other of the groups?

Petty political interests have given rise to attacks, for which no explanation and no excuse can be found.

There is another question which I feel bound to bring before you for your judgement, and this is, the violation of a freedom which everyone has a legal right to enjoy.

I am speaking of the right to express one's thoughts in writing, of which no one, in a democratic regime, can or should be deprived.

In this respect I expressed my opinion when I met the press, immediately after the formation of the government, when I declared myself a determined upholder of the widest liberties for the press, with one reservation, and that was, that dignified and civilized styles should be preserved in writing. I am compelled to state with very great regret that some journalists have ignored my advice, but they may be sure that they have nothing to gain. One part of the press adopts a tone of rare violence and a bearing which is not of a nature to increase the prestige of the press as an institution, whose role is to paramount importance in the education of the people.

If young men, who are still apprentices at journalism, – since they are more inclined to violence – instead of modelling their style on that of notorious Șeicaru, would take example from older and better journalists, leaders of great dailies, they would have nothing to lose, and, on the contrary, everything to gain.

But the return to liberty of press, an extremely disquieting event happened in the course of last week. A number of printers saw fit to take it upon themselves to become the censors of the press. Not only did they refuse to print a communique which did not tally with their political opinions, but they decreed the suspension of the paper, pure and simple. It appears unbelievable, but unfortunately it is only too true.

Can any right-thinking man approve of such thing? Where should we be, if the workers acted like this in every branch of activity? The workers think themselves democratic; they speak in the name of democracy in any and every circumstance. Must they be the ones to suppress the principal attribute of democracy – liberty? What, then, is dictatorship and Nazism? What difference is there between what was done under the Antonescu regime, when everything was written to order, and what the workers are doing now?

Only one source of hope remains; the action of the working printers met with no approval, even among the majority of their comrades, who declare that it was the work of a few hotheads. I trust it will not be repeated, and I take the opportunity of appealing again to the workers to remain in the path of duty, and to give all the support expected of them in these hard times.

A trade union law has been insistently demanded. It has been given. The trade unions are ostensibly trade and professional, not political. Let them therefore look to their jobs and to politics less.

Only thus will they be of any use to themselves and to the country. All agitation mush cease, since otherwise the very existence of the state is in danger. For the satisfaction of political ambitions it is criminal to drive the whole country to disaster.

We can only guard ourselves against the dangers lurking in our path by unity, by the collaboration of all. In the unity of all, without consideration of political creed, lies our only hope.

There will be time enough later for quarrels, for ideological strife, for the squaring of accounts. For the moment there is only room for unity, calm and work.

This is the slogan which must be branded in letters of fire in all hearts. Political adventures must come to an end. We see and feel all the time what the country is suffering as a result of a policy of adventure.

Every good, right-thinking Romanian must rise up against agitation, from whatever quarter it may come.

As far as I am concerned, I again state that, so long as the reins of government are in my hands, I will defend peace and order in the country at all cost, not with the thought of suppressing anyone, but because I am convinced that that is the only road to follow.

In the two months and more of my government, I have, I believe, given proof that I have no preference of any kind for any one of the political groups. (*cries of: That's true!*)

My impartiality and objectivity have been above suspicion. That being so, when I stated my point of view, which I think most fitting for the country's present situation, no one has anything to fear, if he keeps on the straight road.

The agrarian problem. A question regarding which you have to say the final word. This is agrarian reform. I shall discuss in detail the way in which it is to be solved. In my opinion, what is of interest at the moment is the choice of the most suitable time for its achievement. And weighing all arguments for and against, I have reached the conviction that no only is not the moment now, but also that, by proceeding to its realization to its realization now, we should be making a mistake likely to have the gravest consequences. I will explain, in repeating something I have said many times, but which I must repeat, namely that our first care today be the increase of production.

Should we achieve this end now by a distribution of land? On the contrary. All farmers, great and small, would be thrown into a state of confusion. The bigger ones would no longer work their land, the smaller ones would be in a fever of expectation to see what would be given to them. Parts of the land would remain uncultivated, others badly cultivated, and production will fall, not rise.

Let us not forget that at the end of the last war, after the expropriation, a large part of the land given to the peasants remained uncultivated for years on end.

There is another thing we must not forget. Last Autumn, only about a third was sworn of what was scheduled. Can we ignore what is in store for us if the Spring sowing is not carried out as it should be? On the one hand, we shall be unable to give what we bound ourselves to give under the Armistice terms, and on the other hand, utter famine stares us in the face.

There is another factor of paramount importance. We are at the height of the war, and we desire to prosecute the war beside the allies to final victory. The soldiers fighting on the front have a right to priority in distribution. Have the partisans of immediate agrarian reform considered the state of mind of the soldiers when they learn that, while they have been shedding their blood far from their country, their families left at home may remain without land? The fact that I am right is confirmed by reports which arrived only yesterday at the General Staff, announcing that the soldiers demand the postponement of the agrarian reform until their return.

"I beg to inform your Excellency of the following. From information arriving from the front with regard to the state of mind of the troops, it is clear that the great anxiety is felt by the men at the mention in the press of the future agrarian reform, and the various declarations advocating its immediate putting into practice. The soldiers believe that the stay-at-homes will benefit at their expense, and they are afraid that they will be unable to insist on their rights in their absence.

The anxiety and complaints of the troops are all the more justified, as the majority of the men in the front lines are peasants. They claim that the efforts and sacrifices they are making at the front should be taken into account and that they have prior right to grants of land. They are afraid that those who will profit by land grants will be those who have been mobilized for work within the country.

To calm this state of mind, assurance should be given by the Government, through the press and broadcast, that the soldiers' wishes will be taken into consideration.

In view of this serious situation, the General Staff asks you to consider whether it is not better that the problem of land grants, which would react on the morale of the troops at the very moment when they called on to make the greatest efforts of the war, should be studied and dealt with in such way that it should not constitute a further source of anxiety for the soldiers on the front."

The logical conclusion therefore is that agrarian reform cannot, and should not be realized until after the end of the war. Perhaps those who uphold the necessity of immediate reform will be good enough to renounce its application for the moment, since it could only be the cause if grievances which would have the worst possible consequences.

Finally, there are two further questions regarding which I consider it my duty to express my opinion: co-belligerence, and our entrance into Northern Transylvania.

It has been given to understand in certain circles that if the status of a co-belligerent has not yet been granted to Romania, and if our admittance into Northern Transylvania has not been approved, it is because in the key posts of the Government there are no men of standing who enjoy the confidence of the allies, and that another government should immediately be granted co-belligerence and Northern Transylvania.

It is sinful that questions of such importance should be made personal issues.

The status of a co-belligerent, when it is granted to us, will not be a present made for reasons of personal liking. It will be granted because the military help we have given will be recognized as of extreme importance, and because the gallantry of our armies will have deserved it. Our entrance into Northern Transylvania must not be regarded as something to be begged for. Transylvania is ours. No one contests it. We shall enter in Transylvania, because we must.

The statement I have made to you has, of course, been summary, yet clear enough for you to be able to realize the immense difficulties the government is called upon to cope with, and in particular, the difficulties I encounter. But, as far as I am concerned, however heavy and burden, however wearisome the labour, I shall not let myself be beaten as long as God grants me the power to resist.

I have two things to ask of you all:

1. Understanding the difficulty – sometimes the impossibility – of remedying all the shortcomings which each of you come up against at every step. However much good will is shown by myself and my colleagues, the situation in certain cases is such, that there is no solution to be found.

2. Commonsense, the maintenance of absolute order and the harnessing of energy for hard fruitful labour, which is the only way to avoid the

slippery path which leads to disaster. On this point, I must stress the fact that I am in complete agreement with the Allies.

I cannot conclude this address without reminding you of the one among us who, at considerable peril to himself, and with the utmost gallantry, overcome the greatest difficulties: His Majesty King Mihai I.

* * *

Almost every sentence of the speech was greeted with cheers and ovations.

The remarks concerning freedom of the press were welcomed by shouts of: *We Want Liberty! – Long Live Liberty!*

On several occasions the words *King and Country!* and *Rădescu and Order!* were shouted as slogans.

The last sentences devoted to His Majesty King Mihai I were the occasion of an enthusiastic demonstration for the sovereign, and the audience sang the National Anthem.

Document no. 3

National Archives,
Washington D.C. 871.00/3-1345
The United States Mission

CONFIDENTIAL March 13, 1945
No. 152

SUBJECT: *The Drive for a National Democratic Front Government of Romania*

The Honorable
The Secretary of State,
Washington

I have the honour to report upon the campaign of the National Democratic Front for the formation of a government in Romania to comprise only its member parties, the Communists and affiliated organizations, the Socialists, and the Plowmen's Front.

In discussing this question extensive use will be made of enclosures to this dispatch, as indicative of the technique of misinterpreting news adopted by the Left press and also to draw attention to confidential documents of a factual nature relevant to the subject. Some enclosures are in ozalid, while others are sent in three copies.

First Steps Against Rădescu

Ever since the speeches of Premier Rădescu on February 11 and 12, given in my dispatch No. 110 of February 13, the NDF considered that he had taken sides politically and that he was aligned against their group of Left parties. From that time the Left agitation against him steadily mounted, while the National Peasant and National Liberal parties ranged themselves behind General Rădescu.

The shooting at the Malaxa Plant at the time of balloting for a new labor executive committee , which was reported in my telegram No. 130 of

February 21, 4 p.m., brought the political conflict between General Rădescu and the NDF to a high point. Enclosure No. 1 contains two documents discussing the Malaxa incident. Document one, from the evidence available, appears to be a straight-forward account of the event that shows the NDF workers actually began the firing and, significantly points out, that in the plant voting there were but 700 votes for the old communist-controlled committee and 4,500 votes for a new independent committee. In contrast to this account of what local sources agree were actual conditions, document two gives *Scânteia*'s version as expressed in a manifesto of the Bucharest Trade Unions to the effect that "Fascists terrorized the Malaxa workers". It then goes on to say that because of such troubles it is vital for an NDF government to installed in the country.

To the chorus of criticism and Left agitation directed against the Rădescu program, the National Peasant Party paper *Dreptatea* of February 22, editorialized to the effect that dictatorship should never be revived in any form within Romania through the lack of proper respect for liberty and administrative authority. It criticized "useless demonstrations in the streets" and alleged that NDF methods were leading to "disintegration of the people and disaster for the country." The tendency toward anarchy that *Dreptatea* editorial decried appeared as an essential part of the NDF agitation in the campaign for a new government. The above-mentioned *Dreptatea* editorial is attached as document No. 1 to enclosure No. 2.

To further the consciously directed efforts toward anarchic conditions and thus to undermine the government, the Under-Secretary of Interior, whose office had been abolished by a legal decree, transmitted a telegram to all prefects that they should continue to receive instructions from him and that they should not heed General Rădescu.

Coincident with steps of the above nature, there appeared in the Communist press directly Soviet-inspired articles which took the identical line followed by the local Rumanian Communists in their attacks against Rădescu and the bourgeois parties. The National Peasant and National Liberal parties were called reactionary and General Rădescu's program and behavior were strongly criticized. Since the war is not over, the Russian articles claimed it is imperative for order to be maintained within the rear of the Red Army and the political controversy within Romania thus could not be considered solely an internal affair. Document No. 2 of enclosure No. 2 gives translations of sample articles on this subject that had a wide circulation. There is no doubt that he Soviet authorities at this stage were directly behind the NDF campaign and it has been reported to this Mission, on the most reliable authority, that several of the articles appearing in Moscow publications were actually written at the Soviet Legation in Bucharest.

Build-up for the Demonstration of February 24

Following the Malaxa plant incident, Communists began calling for a mass meeting and urging the workers to respond with violence to any attacks upon them. A mass meeting organized by the NDF to be held on February 24, and on February 23 handbills were distributed throughout the town designed to excite the people and to urge them to attend the meeting of protest against the government.

For political purposes, and not wishing to be completely outdone by the NDF, the Peasant Party decided to hold a demonstration on the same day, but at a different place in the city, and to have Mr. Maniu speak. However, on the evening of February 23, the Peasant Party at General Rădescu's insistence to avoid any disorders in the city, agreed to cancel its meeting. Translations of sample handbills regarding the next day's demonstrations are attached as a document to enclosure No. 3.

Coincident with announcements regarding the demonstration, the Socialists and the Plowmen's Front issued statements which showed directly or indirectly that these parties at that moment were united with the National Democratic Front. These are given in document no. 2.

The National Democratic Front issued a series of appeals to every conceivable element of possible support, all given as numbered documents to enclosure No. 3. It appealed to the Army, to the women, to Marshal Stalin, alleged that General Rădescu and Mr. Maniu were planning a Fascist counter-revolution, published statements made by some dissident members of the National Peasant Party, supposedly affiliated with the National Democratic Front, and finally alleged that with the rights and freedom of the people involved it was the duty of everyone to attend the great protest mass meeting. These various appeals are attached as documents to enclosure No. 3 and are interesting because of the various arguments used in each one. To the Army the NDF said they would give better pay and living conditions and also alleged that the historic parties and General Rădescu were sabotaging war production in the factories and thus hindering their fighting efforts. They were asked to support the NDF and to assure a tranquil home for the fighting troops.

Romanian women were asked to support the NDF in order to stop the rise of prices, and shortages, and eliminate profiteering. The NDF even alleged that Rădescu and Maniu wished to deny equal rights to women, and finally claimed that the government by the NDF would mean return of their relatives now prisoners of war in Russia.

To show the country that they were on most intimate terms with Marshal Stalin and were followers of his policies, which perforce must be the best for Romania, the NDF transmitted a telegram to Marshal Stalin congratulating him on the anniversary of the Red Army and twisting the occasion to assure him that their organization would fight against the Romanian Fascists and those sabotaging the "magnanimous Armistice and the historic decisions of the Crimea Conference."

Turning full batteries upon General Rădescu and Mr. Maniu as heads of an organization planning the civil war for the country, the Left press alleged these men had betrayed the people and that it only remained for them "to declare open war on the Allies." The Left criticized the original National Peasant Party plan to hold counter demonstration by declaring it aimed "at the bloody street fighting of civil war." To the Left, Maniu and the Legionnaires were made synonymous.

To fill the opposition's cup of iniquity to overflowing the NDF sought to show that there was no unity within the ranks of the National Peasant Party by prominently publishing a long statement made by an alleged group of national peasants. These dissidents alleged that their party had financed the Iron-Guardist movement and that during the war the party leaders had refused to contact Russia directly, "hoping for a conflict between the great Allies." The Party leaders were also assailed for having joined forces with the "reactionaries of the Liberal Party." For these reasons the "Democratic branch" of the Peasant Party making the statement alleged that the very existence of the Party was threatened because of its inferior leadership and that the Russians had classed the Peasant Party with Fascists. Of course, the only way to change the situation, according to the declaration, would be for the National Peasant organization to adhere to the NDF program.

With the overwhelming propaganda barrage outlined above as a basis, it was possible for *Scâtenia* to publish an appeal to the citizens of Bucharest of all categories to attend the great planned demonstration of February 24.

The NDF Demonstration of February 24

Having succeeded in its organizational efforts to collect sufficient workmen from factories by the use of threats such as loss of pay and jobs, and being assured of a great bulk of passive onlookers attracted by the spectacle, the ceremony began at Piaţa Naţiunii on the afternoon of February 24. A resolution was presented to the demonstrators, attached as document No. 1 to enclosure No. 4, which, of course, was unanimously approved by the thousands of people present in the Square, the spectators or non-participants presumably being included in the acceptance of the motion. This motion condemned Rădescu's government for every conceivable difficulty confronting the country and accused Rădescu and Maniu of "encouraging and protecting Fascist terrorist bands of Hitler's agents." The demonstrators, loosely estimated at 50,000 with passive spectators comprising a sizeable percentage of those present, marched to the Palace Square where the shootings began that have been described to the Department by telegram. It seems clear that the shooting began from the edges of the crowd, from the demonstrators themselves, and the Russian patrol took up the challenge and fired, wounding many. The type of wounds, which were made by pistols of a non-Romanian Army caliber, apparently confirm this. The fact and fiction aspects the whole affair will be discussed at a later point, but after this shooting ceased Mr. Pătrăşcanu, a Communist cabinet minister, reportedly cried out the crowd that "they have shot without shame at the masses of the people. Those who ordered this, those who carried the order out, and those who are really responsible will pay with their heads. From this very moment everyone of you becomes a fighter for the achievement of true democracy. General Rădescu cannot remain at the head of the Government; he must go. An NDF Government must come, for it alone will be capable of weeding out the Fascists."

As the result of firing about the square and in the area of the Interior Ministry, the Russian Command in Bucharest sent the following phrased order to the Interior Ministry at 5:40 p.m.:

"General Moskvitin knows that fire arms were used in the region of the Ministry of Interior, Police Headquarters, Strada Clemenceau and Calea Victoria. Machine guns and hand grenades were used. The Russian command and the Allied Control Commission look upon this incident as inconsiderate and demand that fire should cease at once.

If the Military Command of Bucharest and the Police Headquarters do not take immediate steps, you will bear the whole responsibility. If the firing is not ceased at once, we will be compelled to intervene with our armed forces.

We expect an answer by 18:20 hours."

Later in the evening, at 9 o'clock, a group of demonstrators friendly to Rădescu and Maniu were fired upon the passing trucks in front of the Interior Ministry with the result that again there were many casualties. Other firing from opposite buildings into the Interior Ministry so angered General Rădescu that within the hour he determined to speak to the country and his address, which is attached as document No. 2 to enclosure No. 4, was governed by this indignation. He stated that "handful of individuals" were solely responsible for the disturbances and that Anna Pauker and Laszlo Luca were the prime movers in these disturbances. In a fiery manner he alleged that those responsible for the shootings "have not even the courage of their actions. They will try to throw the blame on those whom they wish to suppress. They dare to throw the blame on the Army which, according to them, is the provoker."

Ascertainable Facts on the Shootings

From the information available to this Mission it appears clear that the Army did not fire the first shots and that when the troops did fire, they fired into the air. Doctors who treated the wounded during the evening stated emphatically to reliable informants that they were made from pistols and other caliber weapons not used in the Romanian Army. An official statement made to the General Staff by the Army is attached as document No. 1 to enclosure No. 5, which from other checked sources, does appear to be the most accurate description of events. Document No. 2 of the same enclosure is a list of wounded given to the Premier that evening by military authorities.

NDF Propaganda

The official version of the shootings as maintained by the NDF appears in the attached communique as document No. 1 of enclosure No. 6. It alleges that the shots came from the Interior Ministry and the Palace and, as a result, General Rădescu is an "executioner and assassin". The country is urged to fight with renewed vigor for a completely NDF government as the only way to stop such incidents.

Scânteia, the Communist organ, carried headlines of the effect that "executioner Rădescu yesterday organized the bloody massacre in the Palace Square." The demonstration was described as being attended by 600,000 persons directed against "Fascists" such as Rădescu and Maniu, who "have taken a position against the decisions of the Yalta Conference." The paper proposed that Rădescu and his clique should be removed and "sent before the tribunal of the people to account for the massacre of the nation to account for the crimes." Taking advantage of omissions of the truth to give a false impression, *Libertatea* of February 27 has an account by the NDF member of the government who said, "only vile liars can assert that the slightest account of provocation or aggression was made by a single demonstrator." He alleged that the shots were fired by the troops in the Interior Ministry and the Palace. This partisan NDF leader stated, "I know how to measure words and I judge facts with moderation and impartially. I was a witness to the events and I say there is no doubt that everything took place according to a pre-arranged plan. General Rădescu wanted to show his strength, to intimidate us, and ordered fire to be open on our peaceful demonstration."

Despite the fact that the Marshal of the Court issued a communique stating that no evidence of any troops being stationed in the palace could be found to justify NDF assertions that the shots had been fired from there and that, on the other hand, two bullets had come into his very office from the "peaceful demonstrators", it was not the objective of those controlling the drive for an NDF government to permit the truth to be known and the communique from the head of the King's Household was censored before publication.

To eliminate these facts, *Scânteia* of February 27, continued to insist that the shots came from the government buildings and "above all from the Royal Palace." Statements throughout the whole Left press tended to distort and falsify the entire proceeding and General Rădescu's speech was called "criminal" and one that "finally unmasks him as a most dangerous Fascist agent and an enemy of the people."

The Left press as well was full of protesting declarations from every possible affiliated organization, sounding the same theme of "Fascist attack", "Rădescu must go" and that there must be an NDF government. *Scânteia* hit the lowest point of the propaganda campaign by publishing in its March issue a purported open letter from General Rădescu's son in which he publicly took the NDF side and placed the responsibility upon his father.

The NDF ministers in the Rădescu cabinet allegedly sent a telegram to the King and copy appeared in the press on February 25, in which they condemned Rădescu and his supporters, urged the dismissal of the government, and the punishment of those responsible for the shootings. This telegram was undoubtedly for political purposes because several days later the King was reliably reported not yet to have received it. A copy is attached as document No. 2 to this enclosure.

The National Democratic Front issued a supplementary communique on February 27, given as document No. 3 to enclosure No. 6, declaring its policy to secure Rădescu's resignation and significantly seeking to deny insinuations that there is any conflict among any of the parties comprising their organization. This was made necessary because of reliable information from the Socialists themselves that the Socialists were not in favor of the NDF tactics and program and were on the point of openly declaring this opposition.

The final element of propaganda pressure coming from the shooting incidents was the very obvious fact of Soviet support, which was given unswervingly to the NDF in all official Russian announcements and local Soviet papers such as *Grai Nou*, the journal of the Red Army. This last paper upheld completely the distorted NDF version of the shootings and declared it vital to purge the state of Fascists and to replace the Rădescu government by one ready to carry out this necessary reform. It had become, said the newspaper, a matter of grave concern to the Soviet Government.

Political Consequences

In the tradition of democratic liberties, the National Liberal Party issued a statement, given as enclosure No. 7, which discusses the entire political problem raised by the shootings as acts of violence and states that the party can only condemn "the setting up of a new dictatorship under the cover of democracy devoid of its essential principles: liberty and order." The party declares its complete support for the continued coalition government as the only means to support the decisions taken by the Allies at the Crimea Conference.

It was obvious, with the pressure of the NDF and the support given by the Soviet authorities, that there was no alternative but the resignation of General Rădescu. As *Timpul* said on February 25, "The tension between the Premier and the NDF, starting with the meeting at the ARO Theatre, reached its climax yesterday. Yesterday can therefore be looked upon as a terminal point and the same time the beginning of new political developments."

The Communists, knowing that the new government had to be formed, called for unity, "but not with the Fascists. Unity against them." On this basis they wished to eliminate completely any coalition government based upon the previous Rădescu pattern. The stage then was set for a completely NDF government with active Soviet support.

Respectfully yours,

Burton Y. BERRY,
United States Representative
in Romania

Annex to Despatch No. 152 of March 13, 1945
National Archives
Washington D.C. 871.00/3-1345

Copy of Lieutenant Magistrate Olteanu's Proces Verbal

Today, February 24th, 1945, 22:30 hrs., in the building of the Ministry for the Interior:

We, Lieut. Magistrate Oltenu Florin, Military Examining Prosecutor to the Court Martial of the Military Command of the Capital, by virtue of the delegation given to us by the Chief Prosecutor of the Military Court, to take part as delegate at the Court of the M.C.C. at the Ministry for the Interior, on the occasion of today's NDF demonstration, report the following:

1. At 10:30 hrs. I reported to Col. Rădulescu, Commander of the Special Gendarme Battalion, and explained the object for which I had been sent by the Military Court.

I explained to the Colonel that his soldiers should in no case fire on the demonstrators, whatever they did, without my being present to try to get into touch with some N.D.F. delegates, if incidents between the delegates and the army had taken place.

Orders to the same effect came from the M.C.C., stating clearly that shots should only be fired into the air and that after legal warning, in order to avert incidents. The orders further declared that if the demonstrators tried to occupy the Ministry for the Interior, the procedure to be followed was according to the regulation of the garrison on duty.

2. Towards 16:30 hrs demonstrators began arrive in ordered columns from the Calea Victoria. About fifteen minutes earlier crowds had gathered in palace Square to attend the demonstration. When the first demonstrators arrived, there was a skirmish round the King Carol statue. I do not know who took part in it, but I could see both demonstrators and public running away and peace was restored immediately.

3. The columns of demonstrators took up their places in groups in Palace Square beginning near the Athenee; as others arrived they took up their places towards the south of Palace Square, so that by 17:30 hrs. the whole square in front of the Ministry for the Interior was almost packed. While the last demonstrators were arriving in the square from the corner

of Calea Victoria, shots began to be fired from the Ilfov Block, from automatic pistols, whereupon the demonstrators began to run away. Believing that the shots had been fired by the troops, the demonstrators also fired pistol shots in the direction of the Ministry of the Interior, and some of the bullets went through the windows into the Prime Minister's study, and into the study of the former Under Secretary of State.

4. Owing to these shots, the demonstrators dispersed – some behind the Ministry for the Interior through the Strada Wilson who tried to enter the Ministry by force. On seeing this the soldiers fired a volley of shots into the air and succeeded in driving the demonstrators away. At the same time, from the Boteanu Block north of the Ministry machine-gun shots were fired on the soldiers on guard at the Ministry for the Interior; (about 20 bullets marks can be seen on the walls, while one of the bullets went as far as the building of the former Ministry for Air and the Navy, where it wounded in the hand and in the eye the soldier ...) as will be seen from the attached proces-verbal.

5. On the failure of this attempt to enter the Ministry by the rear gates, and owing the shots fired from the Boteanu Block, the demonstrators began to disperse in confusion; some went home, others tried to hide, and about a thousand tried to force their way through the front gates of the Ministry for the Interior facing the Palace.

To this end, they forced the gate which was locked and barred, and entered the yard; they went towards the building, although there were notices behind the gate with the words: *"STOP; WHO GOES BEYOND THIS POINT WILL BE FIRED ON WITHOUT FURTHER WARNING!"* Ignoring this, the demonstrators pushed their way into the yard, shouting and threatening the soldiers who were at their posts.

I tried to speak to some of their delegates, or even with Mr. Lucrețiu Pătrășcanu, but it was impossible to come to an understanding with anyone. Captain Teodorescu's Company, in accordance with orders received, then fired a volley of shots into the air, in order to frighten the demonstrators who had thrust their way into the yard. Some of them thereupon withdrew, and I tried to persuade the others to leave the yard and to cease their attempts on the Ministry.

I went to them and talked to two of their leaders; I advised them to get the others outside and to talk to me quietly. I failed to persuade them, and more and more of the demonstrators had pushed their way 30 meters inside the yard. I then asked for the assistance of Major Georgescu, who tried by persuasion and by a cordon of soldiers to remove them. It was impossible.

While I, with Major Georgescu, Captain Ionescu and about a platoon of soldiers, were disputing with the demonstrators and trying to push them towards the gates, in which we were unsuccessful, Capt. Teodorescu's Company fired another volley of warning shots. Some of the demonstrators then fled, their ranks became thinner, and the cordon of soldiers near me pushed them outside and succeeded in closing the gates. We were helped to eject the demonstrators by Russian officer and an English officer.

6. When things were calm here, I was called outside by Mr. Hagiu, delegate of N.D.F., and of Mr. Pătrăşcanu; Mr. Hagiu told me that there were dead and wounded among the demonstrators. I asked him to take me to see them, but he declared that had been taken to hospitals. I had this conversation with him outside, among the demonstrators. I declared that at the beginning the N.D.F. had demonstrated fairly peaceably, but the moment when shots were fired from Ilfov Block at the first disturbances occurred, the demonstrators had begun to insult and threaten and the army and even to fire on them. I assured him on my word of honor that the troops had not fired on the demonstrators, and would not do so, they had only received one order, to defend themselves, and even then they were only to fire after legal warning. I am convinced that Mr. Hagiu believed me and he went away quite as convinced as I that the troops had not fired and would not fire on the demonstrators. Moreover, the casualties could not have been caused by the soldiers' weapons of which the effect would have been much greater if shots had been fired on the crowd of people in Palace Square.

I then re-entered the Ministry building.

7 Speeches were then going on in Palace Square between the status of King Carol I and the Athence. Things seemed to have settled down, when another group of some 500 demonstrators appeared at the main gates of the Ministry and tried to force their way in. Two more volleys of warning shots were then fired into the air, whereupon the demonstrators abandoned their attempt. I must add that both at the first attempt of the N.D.F. to enter by the Place Square gate and at the second attempt to enter by the main gate, Soviet patrols were seen to attempt to prevent the demonstrators from forcing their way into the Ministry; they dispersed them away from the building.

After all these incidents the demonstrators no longer attacked the Ministry, but continued their threats against the army. Moreover, while I was investigating the bullet marks in the wall of the Ministry caused by the shots from the Boteanu Block, I myself saw the demonstrators running after a carriage bearing a high ranking officer and firing four shots after it.

Towards 18:30 Hours – 19:00 hours, the demonstrators withdrew in groups, uttering shouts against the Prime Minister. No more incidents took place.

8. Everything had became calm. At 20:30 hrs., a group of some 500 demonstrators appeared before the Ministry for the Interior and expressed their sympathy for the King and General Rădescu. During their speeches, shots were fired both from the Ilfov Block and from a car, on the demonstrators, among whom two dead and eleven wounded were the results. After they had been identified, the wounded were sent by ambulance to hospitals, and the dead were transported to the morgue.

Conclusion

a. The demonstration proceeded peaceably until the first shots were fired from the Ilfov Block.

b. The NDF reacted against the army, believing that they had fired these shots; this reaction took the form of threats insults and pistol shots fired both on the Ministry and on the Royal Palace.

c. The killing and wounding of some of them was caused by skirmishes and by the shots fired from the Ilfov, Generala, Wilson and Boteanu Blocks on the Ministry and on the demonstrators.

d. The Army did not use their arms until the demonstrators entered the yard and then only under orders.

e. According to instructions and orders received, even if shots were fired, they were fired only into the air in order to frighten to crowd away, particularly as I and major Georgescu were face to face with the demonstrators, trying to get them outside by peaceful methods.

In confirmation of this I have drawn up the present proces verbal in accordance with legal formalities.

Signed: Liet. Magistrate Olteanu Fl.
Military Examining Prosecutor.

Annex to Despatch No. 152 of March 13, 1945
National Archives
Washington D.C. 871.00/3-1345

Proces Verbal
Lieut. Col. Magistrate Dobrotescu Oreste, Military Examining Prosecutor

This day of February 24, 1945:

We, Lieut. Col. Magistrate Dobrotescu Oreste, report the following:

a. Towards 17:00 hours, I received orders from the General Military Commander of the Capital to proceed to the Ministry for the Interior, together with a unit under the command of a captain on active service, whose name I cannot recall; he had received all the orders necessary, while I was to give the legal warnings, if it should prove necessary.

On the way, I asked the officer whether he fully understood his orders, and whether he could tell me what they were, so that I should know in time what I had to do. I then realize that the officer had understood that the troops were stationed in front of the Palace, whereas I had directed the cars with the troops to the Ministry for the Interior, as it was no longer possible for us to go by side streets, we arrived in front of the Ministry for the Interior from the Str. Academiei, where there were many demonstrators, though they were not then demonstrating.

When the demonstrators saw the cars bearing the soldiers, they began to shout. I then got out of the car to order them to withdraw, but they began to shout: "Long live Military Justice, come to see justice done, as the army has come to murder us, who have come unarmed", etc.

In view of this, I explained to them that the troops in the cars were police troops, and that they would not intervene unless the crowd refused to return to their homes in peace and order. The demonstrators, understanding this, began to withdraw. I told the captain in command that it would be better if the troops did not leave the cars, in order to avoid further vociferation; they should wait until I reported on the situation to the Military Command. I entered the Ministry for the Interior to use the telephone, and to obtain information regarding the situation from the prosecuting magistrate officers on the spot, to add to my report.

On seeing me, the Prime Minister called me to report on what was happening outside, and I telephoned in his presence to General Oncică, who, on hearing of the situation, instructed me to send the cars back to the Command.

On leaving the Prime Minister's room, I met Captain Corbu of the Military Command of the Capital, who asked me how things stood. I replied that with a little tact order would be restored. When I arrived outside, I found an uproar because a major of the Frontier Regiment had given the captain in charge orders to get the troops out of the cars. Mr. Gheorghiu Dej, the minister, was there, and I asked him to disperse the demonstrators to avert a real disaster. At that moment a Soviet officer and some soldiers arrived, who agreed with my point of view and asked the Frontier Regiment major to place the troops back in the cars, which he did, and then left for the Command. The demonstrators withdrew in order, and quiet was restored.

To be accurate, the initial mistakes was on the part of the captain commanding the troops, who have not even understood his destination or his itinerary, thus landing in the middle of a crowd which might have been avoided. The second mistake was that of the commanding major who took the troops out of the cars without enquiring about the situation, thus causing an uproar, which died down as soon as the troops had left.

b. Towards 21 hours, when I was in an office near the study of the Prime Minister, who has instructed me to remain throughout the night at the Ministry, a volley of machine gun fire was heard. It was then announced that machine guns had been fired from a car passing along the Strada Academiei into a group of some 500 demonstrators who had been demonstrating for the King and the Prime Minister in front of the Ministry for the Interior.

On hearing this, I gave instructions for the wounded to be identified – I attach the list of names hereto – and to be taken to the Ambulance Station with their cars, which arrived very soon after I had given instructions to that effect. I then ordered the body of a soldier, who had been fatally wounded, to be reported to the morgue of the military hospital. I then asked delegates of the Soviet Military Command to proceed to the spot to check the situation, which they did, in the presence of a Soviet captain.

c. Towards 23 hours a Soviet colonel and a Soviet lieutenant came to the Ministry for the Interior and requested the Prime Minister to go to the Allied Control Commission on a question of urgent and pressing importance.

The Prime Minister, accompanied by the undersigned and by his A.D.C., went to the Allied Control Commission, whence we returned to the Ministry after 01:00 hours at night.

I have drawn up the present proces verbal in confirmation.

signed: Lieut. Col. Magistrate
Dobrotescu Oreste
Military Examining Prosecutor.

Annexes: List of killed and wounded.

List of killed and wounded in the evening of February 24th, 1945, 21 hrs.

A. Wounded

1. Radoslav Radu, schoolboy, 17 years old, of Bucharest Strada Bolintineanu No. 5.

2. Albu Nicolae, policeman, 19th series of Police Div. I

3. Mălăianu (Mălureanu?) Nicolae, schoolboy, 19 years old, of Bucharest Strada Cuza Vodă No. 159.

4. Dobrescu Adam, shoemaker, 28 years old, of Bucharest Strada Evrica No. 19.

5. Fieraru Panait, operator at Tivoli Cinema, 19 years old of Bucharest, Strada Aeroportului No. 27 bis.

6. Banu Gheorghe, stone-hewer, 37 years old, of Bucharest Strada Antim No. 31.

7. Vătăşescu Ştefan, Sergeant of Infantry Gendarmes

8. Abramovici Herman, commercial clerk, 22 years old, of Bucharest, Strada Minotaurului No. 24.

9. Parvescu Aurel, chauffeur, 31 years old, of the Bucureştii-Noi suburb., Str. Cireşoaia.

10. Dogaru Gică, chauffeur, 31 years old, of Bucharest, Str. Ziduri Moşi No. 13.

11. A man only slightly wounded, who was treated at the Ministry for the Interior, and who then went home alone.

B. Killed

1. Ciulea Nicolae, soldier, on whom was found a yellow discharge from the Aiud hospital, made out for destination Bucharest.

2. Engineer Boghiceanu (Gheorghe), inspector, of Bucharest, Str. Caragea Vodă (died in Brâncoveanu Hospital)

Enclosure No. 5 to Dispatch No. 152 of March 13th, 1945
National Archives
Washington D.C. 871.00/3-1345

Report on the Demonstration of February 24, 1945

To the General Staff of the
Military Command of the Capital

From the report drawn up by the Lieut. Magistrate Olteanu Florea, Court Martial delegate of the Military Command of the Capital, the following results are obtained:

1. Total number of casualties:

– Killed among N.D.F. members – unknown
– Wounded among N.D.F. " – "
– Their names " " – "

Among those presumed dead or wounded it is not known who shot, though the houses surrounding the Ministry for the Interior, from where the fatal shots were fired, have been identified.

The nature of the weapon or of the bullets cannot be specified.

Shots were fired from the Ilfov, Boteanu, Generala and Wilson Blocks.

Eye-witnesses: Prosecuting Magistrate Lieut. Olteanu Fl., two American officers, Commanders of Company II and IV of the Special Battalion, Major Georgescu, Commander of the Guard for the Ministry for the Interior, and officers, N.C.O.'s, and men of the Infantry-Gendarme Regiment.

2. Shots were fired as follows:

The first automatic pistol shots were fired from the Ilfov Block opposite the Ministry for the Interior.

After a short interval shots were fired from the roof of the Generala Block.

Shots were then fired from among the demonstrators in Palace Square, and firing was continued from the Boteanu and Wilson Blocks. The victim of the shots from the Wilson Block was identified as the soldier ... of the Ministry for Air and the Navy. (See the proces verbal attached)

Military sub-units on guard at the Ministry for the Interior fired intimidation shots into the air from their places pre-arranges according to the plan of defence drawn up by Major Georgescu of the Infantry-Gendarme Regiment.

Towards 21 hrs., a group of about 4-5,000 people appeared before the Ministry for the Interior demonstrating for order, the King and General Rădescu. A car with the headlights off then appeared coming from the Palace Square towards the Strada Academiei; it slowed down, put on the headlights and shot a volley from machine gun into the demonstrators. At the same time another volley was fired from the Ilfov Block opposite the Ministry for the Interior. The car then disappeared. It is said to have been identified as bearing the number 17094. The occupants of the car who had fired on the demonstrators snatched one of them up into the car, and nothing is known of his fate.

In consequence of these two volley fired from the car and from the Wilson Block, there were two killed and eleven wounded.

The dead were transported to the hospital morgue, and the wounded were taken by ambulance to the hospital.

A copy is attached of the proces verbal of Lieut. Magistrate Olteanu of the Court Martial of the Military Command of the Capital.

Commander of the Special Battalion of Gendarmes
Col. Rădulescu

Military Examining Prosecutor
Lieut. Magistrate Olteanu

Enclosure No. 5 to Dispatch No. 152 from
The United States Mission
Bucharest, Romania
Dated March 13, 1945

National Archives
Washington D.C. 871.00/3-1345

Copy of Address No. 24,696 of February 25, 1945;
From the Military Command in Bucharest,

To the President of the Council of the Council of Ministers

Continuation to No. 32,127 of February 24, 1945

I have the honor to report the victims of the demonstrations of February 24, 1945, as far as they have been identified until 23:30 hours.

1. Ştefănescu Voicu – Commune Viforîta, Dâmboviţa, dead
2. Puşcaşu Nicolae – Railway worker, dead
3. Pascu Ştefan – 19 years old, Bucharest, Şos. Ştefan cel Mare No. 126, received medical care and was then sent home.
4. Dima Angela – 32 years old, had her wound dressed and was set free.
5. Ştefan Piele – mechanic, 39 years old, wounded in the right leg, outside the Ministry of the Interior; belongs to NDF.
6. Tara Bucur – 26 years old, worker at Rudeni-Reşiţa, belongs to the NDF; was wounded in the spinal cord, outside the Ministry of Interior; address: St. Col.Chiriacescu No. 24.
7. Chirica Grigore – 39 years old, Bucharest, St. Constanţa No. 15, belongs to the NDF, was wounded in the leg.
8. Velea Petre – 25 years old, a carpenter, St. Locot. Ganovici No. 52, was wounded in the shoulder, on St. Wilson.
9. Vaida Bella – Hungarian, refuses to show his identity; according to information received, he belongs to the NDF. He has dorsal wound.

*10. Alb Nicolae – constable, seriously wounded in the back and both legs, outside the Ministry of Interior.

11. Stănescu Gh. – 26 years old, married, St. Popa Soare No. 8, tailor, he was shot in the neck.

12. Grigorion Sidorovici – 22 years old, of a military unit, he is a Lieut. He was shot in the leg; 6 mm part of a pistol bullet shell was extracted.

13. Carol Leborix – 32 years old, St. Pascalului No. 88, plumber; a shot wound in the right zygomatic region.

14. Nicolae Iordan – 30 years old, St. Murgului No. 12, founder at Malaxa's, he was shot in the sole; the bullet came out through the fourth toe.

15. Rosian Alex. – 49 years old, St. Dosoftei no. 58, laborer, oval bullet wound on the outside of the right leg below the knee.

16. Luiza Nicos – 34 years old, St. Crângași No. 6, housewife, unimportant wound.

17. Sanda Dumitrescu – 28 years old, St. Dosoftei No. 30, clerk, feel and injured both legs.

18. Dumitrache Ispas – 31 years old, of Ploiești, owner of a shoe-shop, fell and cut his scalp.

19. Patre Toscicu – seriously wounded.

*20. Malureanu Nicolae – high-school seventh grade, Saint Sava College, was shot accidentally.

*21. Dobrescu Adam – seriously wounded.

22. Basil Ladislau – seriously wounded in the afternoon.

*23. Fieraru Panait – clerk at the Trivoli cinema; was shot accidentally, as he was coming out from the office (he told that the shots were fired from two cars).

*24. Banu Gh. – accidentally shot.

*25. Vătășescu Ștefan – sergeant of gendarmes, Machine-gun Comp. shot in the leg while he was on duty outside the Ministry of the Interior (he stated that the shots were fired from the building across the street from the Ministry).

*26. Boghiceanu Gh. – engineer, accidentally shot mortally through the head.

*27. Galbenu Const. – seriously wounded.

*28. Radislov Radu – high-school student.

*29. Ambramovici Herman – commercial clerk.

*30. Pârvescu Aurel – chauffeur

*31. Dogaru Gică – chauffeur

*32. Culler N. (?)

Also we report that shots were fired upon the Royal Palace, the Ministry of Internal Affairs, Police Headquarters, and other buildings. According to information from the lightly wounded, the shots fired from the building opposite the Ministry of the Interior came from the Ilfov Block and from two cars on Str. Academiei. The shots fired at the Royal Palace were fired from the building opposite the Palace.

Military Commander of the Capital
General
ss I. Teodorescu

* Wounded before Ministry of Interior by Fire from passing truck.

* 32. Ciulea Nicolae – soldier, killed, see Oreste Dobrotescu's report (D.C.G.).

Document no. 4

National Archives
Washington D.C., Press General No. 165/1945
United States Mission, Bucharest, Romania

General Rădescu's Appeal to the Country Broadcast on February 24th – 22:00 hrs – from Bucharest Broadcast Station

Brother Romanians!

The nationless and godless, as the people have described them, have begun to set fire to the country and to bathe it in blood.

A handful of individuals, led by two foreigners, Anna Pauker and Luka the Hungarian are trying to subdue the race through terror. They shall fall crushed.

This race, which has always known how to defend itself, will not now be brought to its knees by a few good-for-nothings.

Under the mask of democracy, a democracy which at each step they trample underfoot, these frightful hyenas hope to obtain control of the country.

Their accursed deeds are countless throughout the country. I shall soon have the opportunity of telling you about them all. Tonight I am going to tell you in brief only what happened today, as I wish to dispel all the infamy which has begun to be thrown at me and at the army, in order to hide their odious crimes.

From the information I have so far gathered as to events in the provinces and in the capital, I acquaint you with the following:

In Craiova, armed groups attacked the Prefecture and took it by storm;

In Caracal, the small but gallant garrison stubbornly resisted an attack, so that the Prefecture was able to be saved;

In Brașov they devastated a cooperative store;

Their crimes in the capital will not be fully known until tomorrow.

They fired shots into the Royal Palace, where two bullets entered the study of the Marshal of the Palace. They also fired into the Prefecture of the Capital and attacked the building of the Ministry for the Interior, where I was; a bullet fell near my writing desk. Three-quarters of an hour ago, a group which was demonstrating their sympathy and adherence to me was fired on from a car. There are two dead and eleven wounded.

This in brief is what happened today.

The criminals who perpetrated these crimes have not even the courage of their action. They will try to throw the blame on those whom they wish to suppress. They dare to throw the blame on to the army who, according to them, is the provoker.

I affirm most emphatically that there cannot be more infamous insinuation. The army had my express orders not to attack unless it was attacked. It did even more; wherever the troops were attacked, they shot into the air only in order to intimidate the attackers.

As far as I am concerned, I have done everything in my power to prevent any disturbance. I forbade the mass meeting planned by the National Peasants and I allowed the previously announced N.D.F. street demonstration to take place. The black souls of the nationless and godless however, must needs burden their conscience with further crimes. These are the facts, these are the men. But can we content ourselves with pointing this out without incurring the punishment of God?

Document no. 5

National Archives
Washington D.C. 871.00/3-1545
United States Mission
Bucharest, Romania March 15, 1945

CONFIDENTIAL
No. 158

Subject: *The Formation of the Groza Government in Romania*

The Honorable
The Secretary of State,
Washington

Sir:

I have the honor to report upon various immediate circumstances preceding the announcement of the formation of a Government by Dr. Petre Groza. This dispatch is intended to supplement the material transmitted by telegram to the Department and to continue the description of the efforts of the National Democratic Front, with active Soviet support, to form a Romanian Government of its own creation by excluding the National Peasant and National Liberal Parties.

The Search for a New Premier

The crescendo of NDF and Soviet sponsored agitation against General Rădescu and his Government following the shootings on February 24 all contained the essential statement that General Rădescu's Government must go and that an NDF cabinet should be organized. However, it is noteworthy that the NDF cabinet members did not precipitate an orthodox cabinet crisis by resigning, as General Rădescu requested, but insisted that they would force the premier to resign. General Rădescu had informed the King that when his resignation was desired he would immediately present it. Pending consultations with Romanian party leaders and Soviet officials the King permitted general Rădescu to continue in office while the search for a suitable replacement was made.

It is known that the NDF even considered the possibility of Dr. Lupu, head of so-called Left Wing of the National Peasant Party, being named as the head of an NDF Government, with token Peasant and Liberal Party representation. Anna Pauker, representing the Executive Committee of the Communist Party, personally urged Dr. Lupu to accept a post under these terms, but was unsuccessful, since Dr. Lupu felt the Peasant Party should have greater representation in the cabinet.

An attempt was made to secure a Premier of a non-partisan character and both Prince Ştirbey and General Avramescu, who had commanded the Romanian troops at Budapest, were considered likely candidates. At the close of February Prince Ştirbey was considered the most likely choice to succeed General Rădescu and he was requested by the King on February 28 to attempt to form a cabinet. Prince Ştirbey accepted the mandate on the premises of securing Allied Control Commission approval of his appointment and of NDF collaboration. At noon on March 1st he announced publicly he had failed to secure NDF support. Accordingly, he had so notified the King that day.

Socialist Opposition to the NDF Program

It had been felt that with the support of the Socialists it might even have been possible for the National Peasant and National Liberal Parties to organize a Government without other elements of the National Democratic Front, and *Fapta* expressed this view as prevalent at the close of February. This optimism with regard to the stand of the Socialist Party was based upon the fact that Socialists prior to the demonstration of February 24th and immediately thereafter openly expressed their discontent with the tactics being pursued by the Romanian Communists in the name of all the parties comprising the National Democratic Front.

Mr. Titel Petrescu, the Socialist leader, addressed a letter to the Central Committee of the Communist Party outlining the grievances which his party had against the Romanian Communists. This letter, in English translation, is attached as enclosure No. 1. Significantly, Mr. Petrescu referred to hostility toward Socialist dominated unions in factories on the part of the Romanian Communists. To keep the position of the Left parties intact Mr. Petrescu suggested that the Communists request their members to respect the joint resolutions of October 1944 that obliged Socialists and Communists to collaborate very closely on all political and trade union questions. This could be done by joint committees to control and discuss these problems confronting both parties in order to have misunderstandings quickly adjusted. It was suggested that local workers' commissions should supervise the immediate re-election of all factory and union committees in the event of any present complaint. The necessity for party organizations to cease interference in the trade union questions was also raised. Alleging that the principle of a United Workers' Front, which constituted a working agreement between the Socialists and Communists in trade union matters, was the basis of continued National Democratic Front collaboration, Mr. Petrescu stated that in many cases the principle was not being applied and the NDF was serving only party interests. He objected to the consideration of the NDF as a super party over all Left organizations. Turning to the NDF program Mr. Petrescu urged a bill for immediate legalization of land reform, cessation of press censorship by the operating printers, and regularization of the present methods of local Communists organizations placing in power self-appointed prefects and other local officials.

The significance of this letter and other statements made by Mr. Petrescu actually showed that the NDF as a unified political organization was a fiction. However, competent local observers truly believe that the Socialists had delayed too long in making their opposition public and the Communist dominated campaign for a completely Left Government had gained too much momentum especially when given Soviet support, to be stopped. The Socialists thus found themselves in the position of being prisoners in the NDF movement.

Soviet Intervention

The arrival of Mr. Vishinsky, Deputy Commissar for Foreign Affairs of the Soviet Union, forcefully illustrated the direct Russian interests in the political situation in Romania. The Soviet authorities, led by Mr. Vishinsky, categorically refused any attempt to form a National Union Government with the non-partisan head and demanded that Dr. Petre Groza be named president of the Council of Ministers and Mr. George Tătărescu be named vice-president. Thus all attempts to form a Ştirbey or a Lupu Government immediately fell to the ground.

The political atmosphere immediately following the arrival of Mr. Vishinsky rose to a fever point and the NDF launched a true war of nerves against the historical parties, the King's advisers and in its attempts to influence the public. The King, in view of a virtual Soviet mandate, charged Dr. Groza on March 2nd to seek to form a Government based upon broad democratic and national union lines.

Throughout the entire period from the moment Dr. Groza was named there was a feeling of fatality that the power of the historic bourgeois parties was broken and that the National Democratic Front would strive by every means only to have men acceptable to their organization included in the cabinet. Dr. Groza, for example, wished to name all members of the National Peasant and National Liberal Parties who would be included within his cabinet, whereas the party chiefs themselves, when they finally agreed to cooperate in a Groza dominated cabinet, held out for naming their own men. At this point an interesting statement of Peasant Party policy was issued that is reproduced below:

1. "Mr. Maniu and his party accept neither an NDF government nor a government presided over by Mr. G. Tătărescu, whom they accuse to have initiated Fascism in Romania.

2. The Peasant Party will not tolerate for the time being any other political leadership than a coalition government in which the so-called "historical parties" should possess the same majority as today.

3. They are firmly convinced that, if British and American representatives support the views expressed above under 1 and 2, the U.S.S.R. authorities shall surely renounce to obtain from H.M. the King, by exertion or threat, a decision to the contrary."

The attitude of the historical parties was that the British and American Governments would intervene to prevent any formation of a government contrary to the principles announced at the Crimea Conference and contrary to the Government of National Union that had existed in the country since the coup d'etat. With these convictions, the parties fought for time and refused to make concessions of a significant character to the NDF.

When Dr. Groza was given the mandate to form a government on March 2nd, after the failure of the Prince Știrbey to gain the participation of the NDF in his proposed government, the propaganda barrage in the press through Soviet inspired articles openly stated that a Groza Government of "real democratic forces" was the only solution for the country, to save it from "Fascists" such as Maniu, Rădescu and their associates.

The inclusion of Mr. Tătărescu in the NDF Government was utilized to give color to the NDF picture that the bourgeois parties were not being excluded from Groza Government but that dissidents of his stripe would be truly worthy of representing the Peasant and Liberal Parties.

The day following Dr. Groza's designation by the King as one empowered to seek to form a government, Dr. Groza presented a list comprising a National Democratic Front Government, with several dissident

Liberals and Peasants, not affiliated with the parties of Brătianu or Maniu in cabinet posts, while the overwhelming majority of its members were from the Democratic Front. The King, on March 3rd, was forced to refuse this Government, which in the light of the subsequent constitution of the cabinet is of interest for comparison purposes and is attached as Enclosure No. 2. Substantially the same cabinet eventually was accepted with some deviations more in favor of the Left.

Soviet and Left Press Attitude

The Soviet press, and the local Soviet dominated and Left press, nobly supported the NDF propaganda line for the constitution of a Government and it was possible for *Grai Nou*, the Red Army paper printed in Romanian, to say that "some of the responsible factors in Romania completely disregard realities of Romanian policy by according open support to the Romanian Fascists." The dominant note in *Grai Nou* was that it was Romania's job to eliminate Fascism and to introduce "real democracy". Fascists and legionaries were said to dominate "anti-democratic circles", which presumably included all political elements not within the NDF. Additionally, *Grai Nou* urged purging of the army of its conservative elements, in order that the war could be prosecuted with the assurance that in the rear of the troops there would be no acts of sabotage and opposition in the part of undefined Fascists.

Throughout the whole period while delays in the formation of a Groza government were being expressed it is safe to say that there was one great hope animating the entire Romanian public in contrast to the actions of what must frankly be admitted were those of an NDF minority. This hope was that based upon the Yalta declaration there would be tripartite consultations to maintain a truly democratic coalition government in Romania. This might even be said to have stayed the hands of those pressing for an immediate NDF Government and to have encouraged others to resist any prompt acquiescence to such a minority government, admitted by its supporters privately not to represent the views of more than ten per cent of the population. However, *Grai Nou* also used the Yalta declaration as a basis for stating that it primarily meant that the great decision taken at Yalta was for the Allies "to maintain their unity and to wipe out Fascism and Nazism from the face of the earth." This vital concern in Soviet eyes made the question of the coalition government less essential. *Grai Nou* said that the declaration meant the former Axis satellites should have democratic governments that would not be democracy "distorted by pro-Nazis to the abuse for their own ends of democratic liberties and for the thwarting of the people's struggle against Fascism and the reaction which is akin to it."

Radio Moscow gave able support to every NDF allegation and indeed took the lead as announced by *Timpul* of March 9, that General Rădescu had prepared a new dictatorship for Romania by collecting large military forces in the vicinity of Bucharest and by organizing numerous illegal arms supply depots. The National Peasant Party was alleged to have concealing many legionaries and several of their headquarters were claimed to have been arms depots.

A spirit of pessimism and apathy began to permeate thoughtful Romanian circles when it finally became apparent that an NDF Government would be constituted. As one well balanced and well informed Romanian stated, after the coup d'etat of August 23, 1944, the Romanian people felt that their freedom and liberty would be regained and that real democratic processes actually would be possible to operate in the country. Under the present situation he felt, along with others of his compatriots, that the situation from the standpoint of civil liberties was even now worse that that under the German dominated Antonescu Government, and that with the NDF Government in power the situation would even further deteriorate.

Announcement of the Groza Cabinet

Conference between party leaders, between these leaders and the King, and with Soviet officials, continued during the troubled days until the naming of the Groza Government on Mach 6. The NDF had organized another demonstration for that day, presumably in order to bring the delay in formation of a Government to a head and reliably reported to have every intention, if the King refused to name Mr. Groza and his cabinet choices, to take power by naming such a Government by acclamation in a mass demonstration. This measure proved unnecessary, for as a result of conferences reported to the Department by telegram the King finally agreed to the constitution of a Groza cabinet on lines already laid down in Enclosure No. 2.

The first list of the cabinet as announced in the evening of March 6 later had a few minor changes made and the final list of the new government was given the next day, March 7. This list is attached as Enclosure No. 3. As will be seen from a perusal of the members, there are no outstanding politicians or political figures, except prominent Communists, and the number of dissident Liberals and Peasants given in Dr. Groza's March 3 list was further reduced.

Political Aftermath

The inevitable controversy about the participation basis offered to the historical parties immediately came to the fore and both the NDF and the National Peasant Party issued conflicting communiques on the subject which are attached as Enclosure No. 4. The NDF statement attempted to gloss over the non-participation of true representatives of the Liberals and peasants in the Government, while the Peasant Party declaration states that it refused to participate because Dr. Groza required that he personally approve of their few representatives in his government. The National Peasant Party, following the announcement of Dr. Groza's cabinet, issued a communique attached as Enclosure No. 5, in which it gave its story – one not printed in the press – that agree with the factual information given this Mission by responsible sources. This last communique concluded that the Party would struggle for "the triumph of the free will of the nation, which does not accept this government whose ideology and methods are alien to the soul of the nation."

Dr. Groza in a statement to the press, on March 7, outlined the program of his Government, which is attached in English translation as Enclosure No. 6. He significantly said, with apparent indirect warning reference to the King, that "the will of the people had fortunately been heeded by the Crown and we are happy that these two factors, the people and the Sovereign, have met on the same road. How bad it would have been had it been otherwise."

Respectfully yours,

Burton Y. Berry,
United States Representative in Romania

Enclosure No. 1 to Dispatch No. 158 from the United States Mission, Bucharest, Romania, dated March 15, 1945.

Mr. Titel Petrescu's Letter to the Central Committee of the Communist Party

(Prior to the 24th February 1945)

In a sincere desire to remove once for all the difficulties on the way of the smooth functioning of the United Workers' Front and the National Democratic Front, and in order to make them a reality, the Central Committee of our Party has taken up the problem of our collaboration at this moment which is decisive for the working classes and for the Romanian people.

The Central Committee feels bound to state that, in spite of the fruitful and friendly collaboration obtaining in our central organs, friction and difficulties continue in our local and basic organizations because of the sectarian and even openly hostile attitude on the part of numerous Communists comrades towards our party.

This hostily goes so far that not only is there a tendency to remove Social Democratic comrades from factories, workshops, leading union organs and public posts, but also to arrest them (cases in Olteniţa, Dîmboviţa and Ploieşti) and to threaten them with "deportation to Siberia" and "the Black Maria" (cases in Bucharest Tramway Co., in Moreni, Valea Jiului etc.)

The Central Committee of the Social Democratic Party considers that under these conditions the United Workers' Front cannot fulfill its mission of welding the action of the working classes and of leading the fight for democracy in our country.

We therefore consider it absolutely necessary to put an end rapidly, radically, once and for all, to this situation. It cannot last as it is, and all the more so as the coalition of reactionary forces now aims at striking both of us equally.

In order to strengthen the United Front – to which our Party adhered not for tactical considerations but for consolidations of principle – the Central Committee makes the following proposals:

1. The Communist Party should take the necessary measures to ensure that its members throughout the country respect and apply the decisions and directives comprised in our common resolution of October 2, 1944,

which obliges the members of both parties "to collaborate as closely as possible in all questions of political and trade union interests."

2. Committees of United Workers' Front should be set up, within a short period to be agreed on in common accord, in all localities and particularly in Bucharest in order to decide on all problems of common trade union and political interest, and in order rapidly to settle all frictions and misunderstandings.

The present state of things – when more often than not unilateral decisions are taken, and one side is faced with facts accomplished by the other – must cease, particularly in Bucharest, where certain comrades of the Communist Party systematically sabotage the United Workers' Front. Immediate and energetic measures against those who through intolerance and sectarism sow seeds and strife, thus playing into the hands of the reactionaries banded against the working classes, must be taken.

A permanent delegation, composed of representatives of the two parties must be immediately set up to control the application of instructions in the spirit of the United Workers' Front.

3. No disciplinary measures can be taken against any member of the Social Democratic or Communist Party by any trade union or political organ functioning in the lines of the United Workers' Front without previous investigation and decision of the party concerned, with eventual right to appeal to the coordination committee of the United Workers' Front.

4. As in most cases misunderstanding arise in connection with trade union interests, and as trade union congress did not lead to the general consolidation of the United Workers' Front which had been hoped for, it is necessary to give the closest attention to this very important field of labor.

To put an end to the complains with regard to the unjust representation of our parties in leading union organs, and in order to realize harmonious collaboration in all these organs, we propose that the General labor Confederation should set up local provisional commissions on the basis of the United Workers' Front in every locality.

These local commissions should at once proceed to the re-election of all factory and union committees regarding which either of our parties has any complaint to make. These elections should be made by a presentation of common lists ensuring just representation in accordance with the will of the workers. If no agreement in reached on a common list, the election should be made with secret ballot on separate lists, the respective committee being formed on the basis of the proportion of votes expressed.

The activity of the local provisional commissions must be under the direct control of the local United Workers' Front. When the elections are finished, definite local commissions should be formed through the United Workers' Front by delegations from the unions.

5. It is at the same time absolutely necessary to cease the interference of party organs in trade unions matters, since the union organs, being themselves representative of the United Workers' Front, are obliged to follow only the directions given by the United Workers' Front.

This does not mean the cessation of party work in the unions. On the contrary, it is necessary for delegates of the workers' parties to have free access to the factories for group settings, conferences and any other branch of trade union activity proper.

It is also necessary for trade union organs to order that only the following papers may be freely sold in the factories, namely *Libertatea* and *Scânteia*. This is all the more necessary as in some factories the sale of *Libertatea* is prevented by force by Communist comrades.

6. The principle of the United Workers' Front must be the basis of the National Democratic Front; in many cases this principle is not applied, and the N.D.F. serves party interests.

The United Workers' Front is on principle, and must also be in practice, the backbone of the N.D.F.

Our Central Committee upholds its point of view that the NDF is a form of inter-party collaboration and must not become either directly or indirectly a super-imposed party. Our Central Committee therefore does not agree to the election of National Democratic Front organs by meetings composed ad-hoc, but only to their constitution by delegates from the respective parties. Each of the two parties would thus maintain their individuality of organization and propaganda, since the NDF program is only a program of immediate achievement corresponding to the pressing needs of the country.

The principle of unanimity of voting in taking decisions must be maintained.

Our party will not be able to take an active part in the action of the National Democratic Front if clear directions are not given within a very short time for the organization of the National Council and the National Democratic Front local committees. We therefore propose that a commission be set up to draw up a project of organization charts at once.

7. Concerning the National Democratic Front policy:

a. The problems of prefect, mayors, etc. must be solved at once.

Owing to the sectarism and intolerance of provincial Communist organizations, Communist prefects and mayors have been imposed in all counties where the popular action has been undertaken to change the prefects. They were imposed without regard to proportion of representation or to the principle of the United Workers' Front.

Our Central Committee believes that if this problem is not solved by just distribution of the administrative posts, there can be no fruitful collaboration.

b. *Press censorship* by working printers.

We object to unchecked initiative. Preventing the appearance of the anti-democratic news and articles can only be carried out be the central organ of the United Workers' Front.

c. *Agrarian reform:* a bill must be drawn up immediately and imposed on the government for the legalization of the land grants.

d. Engagements with other parties or people outside the working classes should in no case be made without the consent of the legal organs of our party.

We are firmly convinced that, like us, and particularly in the light of recent experience, you are determined that we should do everything together that is possible for the consolidation of the United Workers' Front. We propose therefore that we should meet as early as possible for the debate and establishing in writing of the principles and directives abovementioned, which should then be communicated, in common, to the executive organs of our two parties.

Signed: Constantin Titel Petrecu
President of the Social Democratic Party
For the Central Committee
of the Social Democratic Party

Enclosure No. 2 to Dispatch no. 158 from
The United States Mission
Bucharest, Rumania
Dated March 15, 1945

Groza's Proposed Government
March 3, 1945

Prime Minister	Dr. Petre Groza	Plowmen's Front NDF
Vice President and Foreign Affairs	Gh. Tătărescu	Dissident Liberal
Interior	Teohari Georgescu	Communist – NDF
Justice	Lucrețiu Pătrășcanu	Communist – NDF
War	Gen. Vasiliu Rășcanu	Communist – NDF
Finance	D. Alimanișteanu	Dissident Liberal
Communications	Gheorghiu Dej	Communist – NDF
Agriculture	Romulus Zaroni	Plowmen's Front NDF
Education	Ștefan Voitec	Social Democrat NDF
Arts	Prof. M. Ralea	Plowemen's Front NDF
Religion	Father Const. Burducea	Pres. of Democrat Priests – NDF
Labor	Lotar Rădăceanu	Social Democrat NDF
Health	Prof. D. Bagdazar	Patriots Union NDF
Social Insurance	Prof. Gh. Nicolau	United Trade Unions, NDF
Propaganda	Prof. Constantinescu-Iași	Communist – NDF
Cooperation	Mircea Niculescu	Dissident Peasants
Industry and Commerce	Petre Bejan	Dissident Liberal
Mines and Petrol	Tudor Ionescu	Social Democrat NDF
Public Works	Anton Alexandrescu	Dissident Peasants
Nationalities	Prof. Vlădescu Răcoasa	Patriots Union NDF
Minister without portofolio	Const. Tătăranu	Dissident Liberal

Under Secretaries of State

Order and Security	Emil Bodnăraș	Communist – NDF
Administration	Ion Burca	Social Democrat NDF
Local Finance	Gh. Vantu	Dissident Liberal

Agriculture	Const. Hagiu	Communist – NDF
Army	Gen. D. Damaceanu	Professional
Air	Gen. Marcel Ionescu	Professional
Navy	Rear Adm. P. Barbuneanu	Professional
War Industry	Eugen Dumitriu	Dissident Liberal
Supplies	Gen. Grigore Nicolau	United Trade Unions, NDF
Education	Aurel Potop	Dissident Peasants
Finance	Mircea Durma	Dissident Liberal
Communications	Ion G. Maurer	Communist – NDF

Enclosure No. 3 to Dispatch no. 158 from
The United States Mission
Bucharest, Romania
Dated March 15, 1945

List of the New Government

Pres.of the Council	Dr. Petre Groza	Plowmen's Front NDF
Vice President and Foreign Affairs	Gh. Tătărescu	Dissident Liberal
Interior	Teohari Georgescu	Communist – NDF
Justice	Lucrețiu Pătrășcanu	Communist – NDF
War	Gen. Vasiliu Rășcanu	Communist – NDF
Finance	D. Alimanișteanu	Dissident Liberal
Communications	Gheorghiu Dej	Communist – NDF
Agriculture	Romulus Zaroni	Plowmen's Front NDF
Education	Ștefan Voitec	Social Democrat NDF
Arts	Prof. M. Ralea	Plowmen's Front NDF
Religion	Father Const. Burducea	Pres. of Democrat Priests – NDF
Labor	Lotar Rădăceanu	Social Democrat NDF
Health	Prof. D. Bagdazar	Patriots Union NDF
Social Insurance	Prof. Gh. Nicolau	United Trade Unions, NDF
Propaganda	Prof. Constantinescu-Iași	Communist – NDF
Cooperation	Anton Alexandrescu	Dissident Peasants
Industry and Commerce	Petre Bejan	Dissident Liberal
Mines and Petrol	Tudor Ionescu	Social Democrat NDF

Under Secretaries of State

Nationalities	Vlădescu-Răcoasa	Patriots Union NDF
Interior	Gen. Stănescu Virgil	Non-Party
	Ion Burca	Social Democrat NDF
	Gh. Vantu	Dissident Liberal
	(appointed today, replaces Atan. Gheorghiu)	
Agriculture	Const. Hagiu	Communist – NDF

National Defence:

Army	Gen. D. Damaceanu	Professional
Air	Gen. Marcel Ionescu	Professional
Navy	Rear Adm. P. Barbuneanu	Professional
Education	Aurel Potop	Dissident Peasants
Finance	Mircea Durma	Dissident Liberal
Communications	Ion G. Maurer	Communist – NDF
Industry and Commerce	Adrian Dumitriu	Dissident Liberal
Supplies	Gen. Gheorghe Nicolau	Non-Party

Enclosure No. 4 to Dispatch No. 158 from
The United States Mission
Bucharest, Rumania
Dated March 15, 1945

Communique of the National Peasant Party

Mr. Petre Groza, asked by the King to form the Government on the basis of collaboration with all democratic forces, has announced the President of the National Peasant Party that cannot offer the Party to collaborate in the government.

He suggested that a few persons of the National Peasant Party whom he personally approves of should be in the government, but without portfolios, only as simple observers.

The permanent delegation of the National Peasant Party has rejected this proposal.

Communique of the Council of the National Democratic Front

During the consultations for the formation of the government, the Prime-Minister, Dr. Petre Groza, suggested to the National Peasant Party and to National Liberal Party that they should name their representatives in the government. They were each offered two or three places in the cabinet.

The leaders of these parties, Messrs. Maniu, Mihalache, Lupu and Brătianu rejected this offer.

Yet, members of the dissident fractions of these parties have entered the government of concentration of democratic forces, formed by Dr. P. Groza.

The Council of the National Democratic Front

Enclosure No. 5 to Dispatch No. 158 from
The United States Mission
Bucharest, Rumania
Dated March 15, 1945

Communique of the National Peasant Party

The National Peasant Party deems it necessary to make the following statement regarding the course of events that preceded the forming of the Groza government.

After the Cabinet under the presidency of General Rădescu had resigned, His Majesty the King consulted the President of the National Peasant Party and told him that, since Mr. Barbu Ştirbey had been unable to form the new Cabinet, He was compelled to ask Mr. Groza to form the Cabinet of coalition of all democratic parties and groups, under conditions that were to be decided upon.

The Committee of the National Peasant Party was of the opinion that His Majesty should not ask the representative of the smallest group to form the Cabinet, since the Constitution demanded that the mandate should be given to the representatives of the most popular party, or to a neutral personality who would be in a position to insure the collaboration of all political parties and groups.

In this spirit, the National Peasant Party as the most powerful of the country, suggested its Vice-President, Dr. Nicolae Lupu, to the King, if He has no preference for any person outside the parties.

The Political groups of the NDF suggested Mr. Petre Groza.

His Majesty the King acted on their suggestion.

Mr. Groza's mandate was limited; he was to form a government of coalition with the democratic parties.

During his first visit to the President of the National Peasant Party, Mr. Petre Groza offered three places for members of the Peasant Party in the Cabinet, but as Ministers without portfolio, as simple observers of the government's activity only.

The Committee of the National Peasant Party rejected this offer.

Mr. Petre Groza presented the King with a list that did not include representatives of the National Peasant and National Liberal parties.

This formula did not meet with the approval of the constitutional factor; Mr. Petre Groza was therefore compelled to offer the two parties a real collaboration, under conditions that remained to be decided upon.

His Majesty The King appealed to the Committee of the National Peasant Party to accept an eventual offer of collaboration, pointing out the extremely serious and dangerous position the country and the Dynasty were in. The Committee told His Majesty that they fully realized the situation and, in order to prove their real feelings, the wish of the Sovereign would be accurately and loyally conveyed to the Forum of the National Peasant Party which would decide.

The Permanent Delegation of the Party decided to accept, in principle, to collaborate with Mr. Groza's government, provided that Constitutional principles are respected, and especially that civic rights and freedom, as well as the loyal functioning of democratic institutions, freedom of the press, of labor, of meetings, etc.

The Permanent Delegation also demanded the immediate expropriation, based on a law, in the spirit of the projected law that the party had already submitted to the Agrarian Commission.

The King and Mr. Groza were advised in due course of the National Peasant Party's decisions.

The second visit Mr. Groza made to the President of the National Peasant Party only took place in March 6, at 14 hours, and then he said he was in hurry and under pressure from the Workers' Meeting in Piața Națiunii.

Mr. Groza did not discuss the essential conditions that were mentioned in the above paragraphs. He said that the Liberal Party had not accepted to collaborate and added that the representation of the parties should ensure a majority for the NDF, and that the Ministry of the Interior, the Ministry of National Defence and the Ministry of Foreign Affairs should belong to the N.D.F.

Mr. Groza's entire procedure made it obvious that what they really wanted was to form an N.D.F. Cabinet but pass it off as a collaboration of democratic forces with the aid of participation of a few renegades of the last minute, as was admitted even by the communique of the Council of N.D.F., and of Mr. Tătărescu, the principal defender of the former King's personal rule, one who was most responsible for Rumania's joining the Axis and for the country's disaster.

The N.D.F. suppressed the freedom of the press by ordering the workers not to print the papers that were of a different opinion and by illegally arresting those who opposed this.

After the public forces were disarmed the N.D.F., with the aid of its armed guards occupied the Public Institutions. They also compelled the workers to help them by demonstrating.

A libellous propaganda, against which we were defenseless since we were unable to print our papers, presented the National Peasant Party as reactionary and lacking in friendship towards one of our great Allies.

This cabinet was formed not only by the above-mentioned methods which strangled national will: pressure of a nature hitherto unused was brought to bear on the Crown itself, which was thus confronted with the alternative of either accepting or abdicating.

The National Peasant Party, faithful to its past, will always continue the struggle for freedom and democracy, with the same faith in its program and its democratic methods as well as with the same loyalty to the three allies, in order to bring about the triumph of the free will of the nation, which does not accept this government, whose ideology and methods are alien to the soul of the nation.

INDEX

A

B

C

D

E

F

G

H

I

K

L

M

Q

R

S

Z